HAPPINESS IS A JOURNEY
SEEKING AND FINDING JOY AND CONTENTMENT

HAPPINESS IS A JOURNEY
SEEKING AND FINDING JOY AND CONTENTMENT

EDITED BY PATRICIA DREIER

A READER'S DIGEST/C.R.GIBSON BOOK

Published by The C.R. Gibson Company,
Norwalk, Connecticut 06856

TABLE OF CONTENTS

Introduction

PART ONE: HAPPINESS IS...
Chapter One Spontaneity

Chapter Two Simplicity

Chapter Three Serenity

Chapter Four Sharing

PART TWO: STEP BY STEP...
Chapter Five Starting a Happier, Healthier Life

Happiness is a journey, not a destination.
Old Proverb

As we travel along the days, some moments stand out with unmistakable clarity—times when our hearts glow with joy and contentment. Often it is hard to define what brings these unique feelings known as happiness. Happiness can be so many things. Spontaneously bursting out of routine in an all-day frolic at the beach with a child. The pleasure we experience when we stop to savor the simple joy of a brilliant sunset or the delicate curve of a new moon in spring. The serenity that envelops us while listening to the soothing tones of Beethoven in the quiet time of a busy day. Perhaps most of all, happiness is that sense of heightened pleasure only known to those who share their joy with others. Happiness multiplies when it is given away.

The path to happiness is a simple one—yet endlessly fascinating to philosophers and writers throughout the ages. On one point they agree: The keys to happiness are within all of us, we have only to learn how to recognize them . . . to learn not so much how to be happy but to discover and tap the happiness that is easily within our grasp.

SPONTANEITY

VOYAGE OF DISCOVERY

"Serendipity." The word sounds like a rare herb or a pale-pink flower. In fact, it is "the gift for making happy, accidental discoveries of valuable things that you weren't looking for." As Columbus might have reported back to Isabella, "Well . . . uh . . . we didn't exactly find India, but there was this other promising piece of land!"

Columbus, in fact, never realized he'd discovered a whole new continent. But the point was (and is) not to go home empty-handed. Life is a disorderly journey. Much of the time we never get where we're going, never find what we hope to find. Yet still, like Columbus, we can stay open to the new and the unexpected. And thus always be ready to discover *something*. Indeed, we can make our entire life a voyage of discovery.

We think of scientists as being orderly folk. But many of the world's major inventions would not be with us today if scientists hadn't kept tripping, falling, fumbling—and then *noticing what happened.* The famous splash of acid on Alexander Graham Bell's pants marks almost the exact moment when the telephone was finally invented. The clumsy spill of gum rubber and sulfur on a hot stove led almost instantly—via serendipity—to Charles Goodyear's understanding, at long last, of how to vulcanize rubber. As Winston Churchill put it, "Many men stumble over discoveries, but most of them pick themselves up and walk away."

Serendipity can be a scientist's miracle, yes, but how do I discover something that will help me make it through a dull Monday at home? How can I "grow" my own serendipity? Here are some rules I have found useful:

Cultivate awareness. "Suppose you fall in love with a girl who drives a blue VW," my son Mark said recently. "Suddenly you start seeing blue VWs all over the place. It's not that there really are more of them. It's just that you are more *aware.*"

The painter Rico Lebrun used to cultivate this awareness by daily walking the 12 blocks from his Los Angeles home to his studio, determined to see something new on every trip—not an easy thing to do. But Lebrun knew what every true artist has always recognized: that you need the new, the surprising, breaking in on you, disrupting you, shaking you up from time to time, if you are to push on, to grow.

Mend your nets. Since serendipity is frequently a side effect of disappointment or adversity, I find myself thinking of our need for "nets"—nets of loyalty, love, conviction, faith, friendship. Such nets must be kept mended so we can bounce back from the slips of outrageous fortune. No one person can possibly be expected to answer all the wants of another. We need many enterprises, too, to carry us through dark nights or gray days when we must be alone. We need to be enthralled by so many different pursuits—interests, sports, avocations, whatever—that we always have another net if one fails us. "When my husband died," a friend of mine recalled, "it was dancing that pulled me through. I'd always wanted to be a dancer, and I found it was still something I loved." The "net" that saved her had been woven years before—and was there to catch her when a sudden blow knocked her off the wire.

Turn your pint into a gallon. "Only what we partly know already inspires us with the desire to know more," wrote William James. He called this "apperception"—masses of ideas already present in the mind through which new experience is perceived and organized.

It's like going to a well to draw water with different-size buckets. Some people have only a "pint" of apperception. Uncurious, they have not broadened their minds; so they can take in only a fraction of what they experience. Other people have gallons of apperception; curiosity and wonder drive them on; they constantly make connections.

Sometimes, when we can barely cope, when we feel trapped or stymied, a "serendipity" suddenly appears and shows us a new path. It's not something we were looking for because we didn't know *what* we were looking for—but in every case *we were looking!* Serendipity comes not to the person who is self-satisfied and uncurious, but to the person who adventures. A hundred adventures that seem without purpose, a hundred miscellaneous interests without immediate value—these are the gallons of apperception in which serendipity thrives.

Trust the current. "There is a tide in the affairs of men which, taken at the flood, leads on to fortune," Shakespeare wrote. I suppose today we would say "go with the flow." Either way, there is something akin to optimism in serendipity, an attitude of trusting the forces of biological life and social circumstance which, after all, transcend us.

Is there a mystical element in serendipity's magic? I don't know. But there have been occasions in my life when serendipity's intervention seemed, if not divine, at least as welcome as a gift from heaven.

My last and most precious instance of serendipity occurred a year ago December. Christmas was upon us, and once again I found it a time of both cheer and sadness. The joy of having three children coming home was mixed with the pain of a fourth child's absence. It had been seven years since Eric died at 22. I miss him every day, but I miss him most during the holidays. On this occasion I was feeling wretchedly low, but still determined to get on with the decorating and the packages. I would leave nothing out: no ceremony, no present, no tinsel or wrapping.

Now I needed one small box to hold a present of jewelry. I had none. It was too late to go to a store, so I hunted. I rummaged everywhere—in the attic, the basement, in drawers that hadn't been opened in months. Then, in my own dresser, I found a box at last. It was the right size and empty—except for a piece of cotton.

I lifted the cotton and there it was: a note from Eric! I'd never found it before. He had tucked it under the bracelet that was his last Christmas gift to me. How lovely that it had been saved for this moment when I needed it so much. In his lively, unmistakable handwriting, the words fairly jumped off the tiny scrap of paper.

"Dear Mom," he wrote. "Thank you for everything you've done for me. Merry Christmas! Eric."

DORIS LUND

How do we become true and good, happy and genuine, joyful and free? Never by magic, never by chance, never by sitting and waiting, but only by getting in touch with good, true, happy, genuine human beings, only by seeking the company of the strong and the free, only by catching spontaneity and freedom from those who are themselves spontaneous and free.

CHARLES MALIK

WHEN IN DOUBT, *DO!*

One winter day several years ago I found myself having lunch at the seaside cottage of some friends, a couple in their 20s. The other guest was a retired college professor, a marvelous old gentleman, still straight as a lance after seven decades of living. The four of us had planned a walk on the beach after lunch. But as gusts of wind shook the house and occasional pellets of sleet hissed against the windows, our hosts' enthusiasm dwindled.

"Sorry," said the wife, "but nobody's going to get *me* out in this weather."

"That's right," her husband agreed comfortably. "Why catch a cold when you can sit by a fire and watch the world go by on TV?"

We left them preparing to do just that. But when we came to our cars, I was astonished to see the professor open the trunk of his ancient sedan and take out an ax. "Lots of driftwood out there," he said, gesturing toward the windswept beach. "Think I'll get a load for my fireplace."

I stared at him. "You're going to chop wood? On this sort of afternoon?"

He gave me a quizzical look. "Why not?" he said as he set off across the dunes. "It's better than practicing the deadly art of non-living, isn't it?"

I watched him with the sudden odd feeling that something was curiously inverted in the proper order of things: two youngsters were content to sit by the fire; an old man was striding off jauntily into an icy wind. "Wait!" I heard myself calling. "Wait, I'm coming!"

A small episode, to be sure. We chopped some armfuls of wood. We got a bit wet, but not cold. There was a kind of exhilaration about it all, the ax blade biting into the weathered logs, the chips flying, the sea snarling in the background. But what really stuck in my mind was that phrase about the deadly art of non-living.

The professor had put his finger on one of the most insidious maladies of our time: the tendency in most of us to observe rather than act, avoid rather than participate; the tendency to give in to the sly, negative voices that constantly counsel us to be careful, to be wary in our approach to this complicated thing called living.

I am always skeptical of claims that the world is getting worse. But in this one area, at least where Americans are concerned, I think the claim may well be true: we *are* more inert than our ancestors, and cleverer at inventing excuses for indolence. Far from burning candles at both ends, more and more descendants of the pioneers seem reluctant even to light a match.

And the disease of non-living can be progressive. A contemporary of mine who gave up tennis several years ago because he feared the game might be bad for his arteries has now taken to going to bed every night at nine o'clock. He says he needs his rest; and, to be fair, he does look remarkably rested. But you can't help wondering what he plans to do with all the energy he's conserving.

The march of science has handed us such bonuses in health and energy and life-span that we should be living hugely, with enormous gusto and enjoyment, not tiptoeing through the years as if we were treading on eggs. For thousands of decades, man's chief concern was simply how to survive. Now the crucial question has become not how to stay alive but what to do with a life that is practically guaranteed.

The whole thing hangs on a series of decisions each of us is constantly called upon to make, decisions that spell the difference between living and non-living.

As a youngster I remember being given a solemn bit of advice supposed to apply to almost any situation: "When in doubt, don't." Well, perhaps this cautious approach has occasional value as a brake on the impetuosity of youth. But its usefulness diminishes rapidly once you're past 20. It can be dangerously habit-forming after 30, and after 40 it probably should be reversed altogether, becoming: "When in doubt, do." If you keep that formula in mind, the problems of non-living are not likely to become much of a threat.

On my desk lies a letter from a friend, a clergyman: "The trouble with most of us," he writes, "is lethargy, absence of caring, lack of involvement in life. To keep ourselves comfortable and well-fed and entertained seems to be all that matters. But the more successful we are at this, the more entombed the soul becomes in solid, immovable flesh. We no longer hear the distant trumpet and go toward it; we listen to the pipes of Pan and fall asleep."

And he goes on wistfully: "How can I rouse my people, make them yearn for something more than pleasant, socially acceptable ways of escaping from life? How can I make them want to thrust forward into the unknown, into the world of testing and trusting their own spirit? How I wish I knew!"

There's only one answer, really. Each of us must be willing, at least sometimes, to chop wood instead of sitting by the fire. Each of us must fight his own fight against the betrayal of life that comes from refusing to live it.

Every day, for every one of us, some distant trumpet sounds—but never too faint or too far for our answer to be: "Wait! I'm coming!"

ARTHUR GORDON

THE BEST DAY OF OUR LIVES

Newly divorced, with a seven-year-old son to support, I attempted recently to re-enter the teaching profession I had left when my child was born. As the job hunt stretched into weeks, however, I experienced a growing sense of panic. But one of the things I have learned in becoming suddenly single has been to reach out to good and gentle friends. One of them shocked me when he said I worried so much about the future that I had no time to enjoy the present.

"Go ahead and look for your job," he said. "But live in the now. Perhaps this time is a gift, one that may never be given again. Use it to discover who you are and what it is that is really important to you."

I began to see, just a little bit, what I had been doing to myself, what I have been doing all my life. Living in the future. Never really being present in my own here and now. What a thief I had been—stealing from myself. And I had absolutely no idea of how to change.

I searched my heart and memory for origins of the "work now, live later" ethic. And for the beginnings of the deeply held belief that if I was not actively productive in a way that was immediately visible—either in a paycheck, or a shiny floor or a possession—then I was somehow unworthy. Perhaps, I finally decided, the important thing is the awareness, and the opportunity to become free, just a little bit.

That afternoon, I thought about Steven, and wondered how long it had been since I had taken time to be *truly,* fully, with him.

When Steven returned from school, I offered to play some

of his games with him. He had tried to get me to play many times but I always had something "more important" to do. He got out the games and I noticed immediately that every one of them was somehow linked with achievement. How many points scored, words made, and in the least amount of time? And don't forget to keep score. So we are teaching it to them, too, I thought.

I suggested to Steven that we might play without the score cards. After his initial shock, and even reluctance, he agreed. Eventually, we even progressed to the point where we were able to make up our own words—though they were not in the dictionary—and to laugh at our own inventiveness. The experience left me hungry for more.

At Steven's bedtime, I said to him: "Honey, we haven't had much time together lately. You and I ought to just go off on an adventure. I just might show up at your school one morning, and steal you away for the day."

Steven's face registered surprise, then impish delight. "Oh, make it a Thursday, Mommy. We have book reports on Thursday, and I hate book reports."

Two weeks later, I got to the school as California's December-morning coolness was beginning to dissolve into warmth. When I entered the classroom, Steven eyed me calmly, but his teacher looked incredulous when informed, without explanation, that my son would be leaving for the day. I merely smiled and hoped the delicious sense of mischief in my heart was not evident in my eyes.

Looking sober and serious, Steven and I made our way safely into the parking lot, where we laughed until tears came streaming. Quickly, we made our getaway. I had packed everything that we might need—lunches, snacks, books, soft drinks, bathing suits, beach balls, warm jackets.

We turned off the Pacific Coast Highway, coming to a halt in front of gently rolling waves that sent white foam bursting on brilliant sunlit sand. Except for about 50 large seagulls and two men, a woman and a little girl, the beach was entirely ours. Steven changed into his swimming trunks and was in the water before I could even spread the towels and snuggle down with a book.

The little girl, attracted by Steven's beach ball, joined us in digging deep holes and tunnels in the sand. The child's father introduced himself and his party. They were Sioux Indians, he said. This was their first day in California and the very first time they had seen the ocean. They taught us the Sioux words for perfect day and beautiful children. Steven taught them the word Kool-Aid.

Then our visitors left. As I lay back on the sand and saw that little boy who is so special to me, really saw him, rushing out to meet the foaming waves, and heard his laughter and basked in his and in my own deep pleasure, my only regret was that I had not brought my movie camera. What I didn't know in that moment is that I will be able to run that scene over and over for as long as I live.

Later, we made footprints in the sand and wrote our names again and again, and laughed as the waves washed away all traces of our being there. We climbed rocks. We found a friendly dog and some fossils. We met a boy and a girl having a picnic lunch and asked them if they were playing hooky, too. They laughed; we all laughed.

The day seemed to flow from one good thing into another. When at last the breeze became cool and the sun fell a little and our stomachs told us that it might be time to have another meal, Steven ran to me with his new treasures — seaweed, shells, bits of pretty rock — and said, "Mommy, do we *have* to go home?" There seemed to be a question beyond the words.

"No, Steven, let's drive down the beach to that restaurant with the big old booths in the windows, right smack on top of the waves."

As we were seated, with the surf pounding only a few feet below, we noticed a man running and jumping over the giant rocks that were covered with moss and looked to be slippery. He had only a few sandpipers, the wind and the sunset for companions.

From the next booth, we heard a man exclaim, "Look at that nut out there hopping on the rocks. And it's almost dark!"

Steven looked at me and smiled. After a while, he said softly, "I bet there are things some people just don't know about."

My son fell asleep in the back seat of our car on the way home. I could hear his soft snoring. When I carried him into his bedroom, he awakened and said, "Oh, Mommy, this has been the very best day of my life."

"Mine, too, Steven dear," I replied. "Mine, too."

COLLEEN HARTRY

No matter what looms ahead, if you can eat today, enjoy the sunlight today, mix good cheer with friends today, enjoy it and bless God for it. Do not look back on happiness — or dream of it in the future. You are only sure of today; do not let yourself be cheated out of it.

HENRY WARD BEECHER

APRIL ANSWERS...

This is the season when I can listen only so long to a recital of the world's shortcomings. Then I must go out, and see the world itself. Last night I heard a long harangue by a man who is full of the world's ills, and today I took a walk up the mountainside and found that though a hundred things may be wrong, a thousand things are right and completely in order.

Water still runs downhill, making brooks that sing and rivers that flow seaward. Grass still sends up green shoots in the pasture. Robins strut on the lawn and sing their mating call from the trees. Daffodils come to blossom. Maples begin to open wine-red bloom.

The world is all right. The ills are among men. April invites a conference on the open hillside to investigate the state of affairs at their common source.

HAL BORLAND

A CONSTANT JOY

Everybody needs an activity that makes him feel like a kid again.

You can see the enthusiasm in the eyes of a runner who has crossed the finish line, accompanied by the cheer of the crowd. You can see it in the eyes of a hunter who impatiently awaits opening day and dreams of that record hunt. You can see it in the eyes of a homemaker making rugs—a pastime she has enjoyed for decades. Maybe you hear a sparkle in the voice of a long-distance biker or perhaps there's just a murmur of pride in the comments of a woman who has made her favorite bread for a bake sale.

Everybody has a special gift. Those who take advantage of it have a constant source of joy.

LESLIE SATRAN

THE SECRET OF HAVING FUN

Studying for his doctor's degree in psychology some years ago, my husband decided that he needed relaxation, and tried to teach himself to play the recorder. He struggled grimly for several evenings with scales and "Three Blind Mice." Then he gave up. "Too much like work," he said, and went back to his books. Our four-year-old daughter discovered the instrument one morning on his study bookshelf. Holding it up expectantly, she put it to her lips and blew a high, quavering toot. Delighted, she skipped out into the sunshine, improvising a melody as she went along. My husband said to me later, "The moment she made that ridiculous sound, I knew she was playing the recorder as I had longed to—just playing it and having fun!"

All too often we adults work so hard at our "fun" that we really don't enjoy ourselves at all. In fact, couldn't the real cause of much of our fatigue, tension and anxiety be as simple as this—we've forgotten how to play? As a psychologist and consultant on family-living problems, time and again I've heard the unhappy questions: Where did the magic go? What happened to the joy in life? How can I recapture the thrill of being alive? And after years of studying and observing young children—children at play—I'm convinced that they have the answers.

What's the secret? Part of it is that a child doesn't ask if what he's doing is worthwhile. He plays for the sake of play, as an end in itself.

When we adults want to enjoy ourselves, we almost always seek to be entertained by others—or we fall back on things that provide us with a kind of programmed play: cards, bowling balls, golf clubs. We let places and objects tell us what to do, how we should react.

When a child plays, *he* is the manipulator; he makes do with whatever is at hand. His imagination transforms the commonplace into the priceless. A wooden clothespin, rescued from under the kitchen table and wrapped in a dishcloth, becomes a baby; a penny thrust under a cushion becomes a buried treasure. As we grow older and "wiser," we lose this talent.

What can we do to regain this lost capacity for play, for make-believe? Here are some of the things that children teach us:

Be alive to the moment. Study the absorption on a child's face as he sails a feather through the air, or rolls a potato across the floor into a dustpan. For him the moment is everything. Without conscious thought or plan, he brings to whatever he is doing spontaneous — and infectious — joy.

There is in children's play a fresh and quite lovely quality of freedom, of "letting themselves go." And we adults will find that something wonderful happens to us when we "let go" of our grown-up self-consciousness. A father of four told me recently how one night, after a frustrating day at work, he found himself becoming increasingly annoyed by the playful antics of his children's dog, who wouldn't let him alone. Finally he took the dog outdoors. "The air was fresh and cool, and suddenly something snapped! Before I realized what I was doing, I was playing with that dog like some kind of a nut. We chased each other around the lawn; I'd throw sticks and then we'd race to see who could pick them up first. Afterward it took me 20 minutes to catch my breath — but it was the first night in months that I didn't feel half-dead when I went to bed."

Be flexible. Don't be rigid about what seems sensible. A child feels no compulsion to continue an activity beyond the moment when it ceases to give him pleasure. He's ready for any new adventure, anytime. We, however, grow ashamed of being spontaneous. If we are at home doing the family wash or at the office writing the monthly sales report, and suddenly a warm breeze through the window makes us dizzy with the thought of spring, what do we do? We tell ourselves that the schedule must be kept.

Giving in to one's impulses for a few minutes does *not* automatically lead to lazy irresponsibility. Quite the reverse: it can lead to greater efficiency and productivity, for it refills the reservoir of self and nurtures an inner core of being that needs to be lovingly refreshed.

Whenever our daughter is feeling especially exasperated with us, she reminds herself of one of the happiest evenings of our lives. About midnight of a school night my husband and I ended a discouraging discussion about money. It had had its usual effect — we were ravenous, not for anything ordinary, but for chicken supreme at Sardi's. We awakened Wendy, age 12, from a sound sleep, something we'd never done on impulse before. She wasn't a bit surprised. "I'd love it! Can I wear my velvet party dress?" So the three of us piled into a cab, drove to the restaurant and blew the last of our bankroll.

Renew your ties with nature. Caught as many of us are in concrete boxes on concrete streets, we lose contact with our roots in nature. We need to find and invent ways to keep in touch with sky and sun and sea. Children understand the sacredness of these things. They are absolutely sure that the world is full of remarkable and exciting things to see and do, to taste, touch and feel. They respond with their senses to the miracles of the natural world. When they tug you outside by the sleeve, give in. Follow them. Join them for a walk in the woods; lie down with them in an open field, look up at the sky and chew on a piece of grass. For a moment, see the world through their eyes.

Reach back for the child within you. It is not by accident that stories of young lovers describe them going on picnics, running barefoot down a beach, visiting a zoo or eating ice cream cones on a carrousel. When we begin to fall in love, we know instinctively that somehow we find our truest selves in the playful games of childhood.

About a year ago I happened to notice a toy horn in a music store, each note hole marked in a different color. With it came a booklet of tunes in which all the notes were written in the corresponding colors. My husband's favorite Christmas carol was in the book. *Eureka!* I thought. *Here is an instrument that he can play without work.*

It was the best present I ever gave him. Now, in the hallowed halls of a great university, one can sometimes hear the high, squeaky sounds of "Good King Wenceslas" as a psychology professor, resting from his teaching and research, fills his office with the only music he can make—on a toy horn, with colored notes. He is one of the rare and fortunate grownups who have watched a child play and learned a precious lesson about living.

EDA J. LESHAN

Enthusiasm is the electricity of life. How do you get it? You act enthusiastic until you make it a habit. Enthusiasm is natural; it is being alive, taking the initiative, seeing the importance of what you do, giving it dignity and making what you do important to yourself and to others.

GORDON PARKS

SIMPLICITY

MIRACLES

Why, who makes much of a miracle?
As to me I know of nothing else but miracles,
Whether I walk the streets of Manhattan,
Or dart my sight over the roofs of houses toward the sky,
Or wade with naked feet along the beach just in the edge
    of the water,
Or stand under trees in the woods,
Or talk by day with any one I love, or sleep in the bed
    at night with any one I love,
Or sit at table at dinner with the rest,
Or look at strangers opposite me riding in the car,
Or watch honey-bees busy around the hive of a summer
    forenoon,
Or animals feeding in the fields,
Or birds, or the wonderfulness of insects in the air,
Or the wonderfulness of the sundown, or of stars shining
    so quiet and bright,
Or the exquisite delicate thin curve of the new moon in
    spring;
These with the rest, one and all, are to me miracles,
The whole referring, yet each distinct and in its place.

To me every hour of the light and dark is a miracle,
Every cubic inch of space is a miracle,
Every square yard of the surface of the earth is spread
    with the same,
Every foot of the interior swarms with the same;
Every spear of grass—the frames, limbs, organs, of men
    and women, and all that concerns them,
All these to me are unspeakably perfect miracles.

To me the sea is a continual miracle,
The fishes that swim—the rocks—the motion of the
    waves—the ships with men in them,
What stranger miracles are there?

WALT WHITMAN

The happiness of life is made up of minute fractions—the little, soon forgotten charities of a kiss or smile, a kind look, a heartfelt compliment—countless infinitesimals of pleasurable and genial feeling.

SAMUEL TAYLOR COLERIDGE

THE THINGS THAT COUNT...

"Teach us delight in simple things," wrote Rudyard Kipling years ago. Today, in our fast-paced world, we might add, "And help us simplify our lives to make room for them."

One evening I got home at 5:30 feeling tense and rushed. I was late starting dinner, and my husband and I planned to attend an early meeting.

At that moment, the lights went out—all over the neighborhood.

It was November 9, 1965, the night a great power failure darkened much of the northeastern United States. My teen-age daughter and 12-year-old son and I had no idea what had happened. Only when we turned on the car radio did we learn. "I guess Dad won't be out from the city for a while," my daughter said. "The trains aren't running." So, we would be more rushed than ever...

But then I realized, with relief, that there would be no meeting if the blackout continued. I began to relax. Our spirits rising, the children and I found candles and lighted them. We made a fire, cooked hot dogs on a stick.

Without the distractions of radio or television, Andrea and Brad settled down right after supper to study by candlelight. I browsed through a beloved book of poetry I had been "too busy" to look at for years. My husband, Russ, got a ride out from the city and joined us happily in our cozy lair.

Later, after the children had gone to bed, Russ and I lingered by the fire, watching castles in the coals, reluctant to give up this unexpectedly lovely evening. "Do you suppose it could be like this more often?" he asked me wistfully.

"Of course," I assured him. "We'll just make an effort, and—"

"Maybe what we need is to make *less* effort," he suggested thoughtfully. "That meeting we were going to tonight, for example—we had nothing to contribute to it. We merely thought we should show up. I wonder how much of our time we fill with things that don't count—things not important enough to justify the effort we spend on them."

Was it possible that if we slowed down the merry-go-round we might take new delight in the scenery? I decided to try.

Next morning, facing a complicated melange of errand-running, drawer-straightening, silver-polishing, I realized that although November was more than a week old, I had not driven once into the countryside, as I loved to do in autumn. On impulse, I got in the car and headed north. The drawers would wait, but not the last golden leaves; not the bittersweet, nor the red berries of dogwood.

We Americans are inclined to overcomplicate happiness—and to risk losing it in the process. We deceive ourselves with countless pursuits that *should* be fun—the book we *should* read, the play we *should* see. Like the legendary opera-goer who mutters, "I'm going to enjoy this if it kills me," we tend to force so-called pleasure upon ourselves as though it were punishment.

We sometimes forget, as we grow older, the magic that is all around us. We let petty distractions blur our vision of enchantment. "Life is frittered away in detail," Henry Thoreau wrote. "Simplify, simplify..."

We have friends whose marriage was in grave danger last summer. They were quarreling increasingly; their one hope was that a vacation away from the city might bring them closer. Looking in the paper, they found an ad for a summer rental that sounded ideal: "Choice location, desirable road, all conveniences, easy living—"

When they went to see the place, they could hardly believe their eyes. It was a ramshackle old house at the end of a tiny dirt road in the middle of nowhere. The inside, although clean and neat, was downright primitive.

"What is this?" our friends stammered to the genial, pipe-smoking owner. "You advertised conveniences—location—desirability—"

"Yes, sir," the old man replied proudly. "You'll go a long way to beat this place for them things. Why, look out there! No main road for miles around. Sleep like a log, no traffic noises. As for conveniences—you got a broom, a couple of pots, and a stove that don't hardly work. No chance for heavy house-keepin'. No chance for gardenin', either—it's berry bushes and roses all over the garden, gone wild. That's what makes the livin' so easy," he beamed.

On a wild impulse our friends decided to take the house. They wrote us, saying no doubt they would be bored and back in town within a week.

But they did not come back. Halfway through the summer, we received a surprising letter from them, describing their life in that little house. They told us how they sat together on the porch in the evening, under the scramble of sweet-blooming roses, and talked—because there was nothing else to do. "We haven't talked like this in years."

The best news of all was scrawled large at the end of the letter. "We never would have thought of leaving each other if we had got *really* acquainted before. . . . Bless this house."

Bless any house where the things that count are not pushed out by those that don't.

Years ago, newly arrived in a strange town, I was invited through a friend to a dinner party at the home of a woman famed locally as a hostess.

At my ring, the door was opened by a casually dressed, merry-faced young woman who put me at ease at once. "Come on out to the kitchen and keep me company," she urged. In the kitchen I found six other guests: one was making a salad, others were carrying dishes out to a prettily set table on the terrace. Before I knew it, I was pitching in, chatting and laughing with the others.

The dinner was delicious, the conversation gay. After we had eaten, Elsa, our hostess, brought a record player out to the terrace. Smiling, she asked us to listen "with our whole selves," and played a record of haunting flute music.

We gave ourselves up to the sweet thread of sound. Gradually we became aware of the flower scents from the garden, the slow upward sail of a great white moon, a gathering intensity of stars; of the night, the magnificent night of summer.

When the music ended, we resumed a soft conversation, our companionship strengthened by the rare experience we had shared.

"What a magical evening Elsa has given us," I murmured to one of the other guests.

"She always does," he answered. "Elsa understands the simplicity of joy."

The simplicity of joy...a precious understanding, and one which can belong to anyone, rich or poor, young or old. As Robert Kahn puts it in his book *Lessons for Life:* "When life is spent and all added up, what are the memories that warm our hearts? The happy laughter of a child as we swung him high; the joys of an after-dinner hour when we put aside the dishwashing for a bit and just sat and talked; the movie we saw together and the ice cream we enjoyed after it."

Fleeting fragments of wonder that can come to every one of us — delight, delight in simple things.

ELIZABETH STARR HILL

SIMPLIFY YOUR LIFE!

Successful living, says this distinguished thinker, is an endless quest for the simple, the clear, the true.

"I must strip my vines of all useless foliage and concentrate on what is truth, justice and charity," wrote Pope John XXIII in his *Journal of a Soul.* "The older I grow, the more clearly I perceive the dignity and winning beauty of simplicity in thought, conduct and speech; a desire to simplify all that is complicated and to treat everything with the greatest naturalness and clarity."

John's simplicity gave his actions the force of parables. As Pope from 1958 until 1963, he was driven by one grand and simple idea: peace. He was a reconciler. His Catholic people had stood apart from Jews for 19 centuries; but when Jewish leaders visited him he did not quote intricate doctrines to overcome the distance. He simply acted out the Bible story of a man separated from his family. John reached out to his visitors and said, "I am Joseph your brother."

All the truly deep people have at the core of their being the genius to be simple or to know how to seek simplicity. The inner and outer aspects of their lives match; there is something transparent about them. They may keep the secret of their existence in a private preserve, but they are so uncluttered by any self-importance within and so unthreatened from without that they have what one philosopher called a certain "availability"; they are ready to be at the disposal of others.

Part of genius *is* simplicity, in the sense of oneness of life, of gathered force. We sense an affinity between Albert Einstein's admiration of childlike simplicity and his own powers of wonder and concentration. We sense a connection as well between simplicity and profundity. Albert Schweitzer was musician, philosopher, historian, physician; but his profundity lay in one simple idea, the focus of his years of service in Africa: reverence for life.

Successful living is a journey toward simplicity and a triumph over confusion. Many use the term "spirituality" to describe the route for this journey. Some cherish a spirituality of ecstasy. Like the prophets and mystics, they find their center in God, in the All. They reach a sudden enlightenment that re-orders their lives. Others experience a spirituality of agony, on the more barren landscape of loneliness and doubt. But it, too, can give clarity to life. And activists possess what I call spirituality materialized; we see it in Schweitzer and others who change the world.

In all these approaches the common thread is the genius to be simple. Dietrich Bonhoeffer, a pacifist who was in on the plot to kill Hitler, tried to explain before he died on Nazi gallows how simplicity can be one's guide. "To be simple," he wrote, "is to fix one's eye solely on the simple truth of God at a time when all concepts are being confused, distorted and turned upside down. It is to be single-hearted."

Even when genius explains itself, there is force, there is unity, in an underlying simplicity of thought. Karl Barth, the Swiss theologian, was another who saw clearly during the Nazi era. The world could not corrupt his faith. Asked years later by an American audience to summarize the gist of his enormous books on theology, the learned man charmed them by quoting from a Sunday-school song: "Jesus loves me, this I know, for the Bible tells me so."

What assets await those who achieve this inner grace? French mystic François Fénelon wrote, "When we are truly in this interior simplicity our whole appearance is franker, more natural. This true simplicity makes us conscious of a certain openness, gentleness, innocence, gaiety and serenity.''

Though the search for simplicity is, at any time, a difficult journey through a wilderness, we can learn from guides ancient and modern. In a way, the American sect called the Shakers had the right idea when its members sang of the ''gift to be simple.'' It often looks like a grace to be enjoyed more than a goal to be sweat over. Nature is not stingy with this gift, but it exacts some effort, so the Shakers called for a conscious act, a need to ''turn, turn.''

People who despair because their calendars are so crowded and their duties demanding have to turn, to put a premium on simplicity. Some find a way by clearing a special room and a certain hour in which they can strip away what matters finally in their lives from all the things they have to take very, very seriously — but in the end not *too* seriously.

The guides on this journey advise others to follow exemplars. Some find them through reading; the religious may do it through meditation and prayer; the thoughtful often keep journals of their souls' journey.

In Western culture more people claim to find simplicity in Jesus of Nazareth than in any other figure. Scholars have written millions of books about him, but people first followed him because they saw in Jesus a life covered in five words: ''He went about doing good.'' Those who admire a modern such as Mohandas Gandhi know that the great Hindu leader was a cunning politician who upset empires, but they see how he focused his life with passion on people he called ''the last, the least, the lowest and the lost.''

The lives of such leaders offer clues, not codes, for the simple way. Each individual has to discover and nurture the appropriate path for himself. Searchers often band together for the journey. Some have tried communes, only to find them complicated. Others have found both freedom and communion in congregations, clubs or causes.

Sooner or later, the searchers learn to live in harmony with nature. But the genius of simplicity has to do with more than the material world, so the seekers have to prune and sort ideas until the lasting ones alone survive. At this point they come to a crucial step; they learn to be suspicious of simplism. The advice of English philosopher Alfred North Whitehead to natural scientists is well placed for all thinkers: "Seek simplicity—and distrust it."

I came to this theme while writing a history of 500 years of American religion. Wherever I have looked in the national past it became clear that citizens use faith to simplify life. Modern American existence is especially bewildering, but we still have to endow our joys and sorrows with meaning, refusing to let them "merely happen." Millions turn to the life of the spirit to sort out the complexities of life. This search for order and simplicity is a constant in religion and may be close to a definition of it.

Simplicity does not call for anyone to turn back to the good old days, or even back to nature. And true simplicity demands no commune or cult. For most of us it will mean life in the company of others who can judge us and nudge us. In community we can follow the trajectory of our belief and develop the core of our being.

One man who was on the path of true simplicity was, according to the Talmud, a certain Rabbi Zusya. He once said, "In the coming world, they will not ask me: 'Why were you not Moses?' They will ask me, 'Why were you not Zusya?'"

MARTIN E. MARTY

HOW TO GET A LOT OUT OF A LITTLE

Properly cultivated, small moments grow into big ones.

The happiness that floods you when for an instant you glimpse your children, not as parts of a domestic frieze but as free-standing beings. The absolute sense of completion that follows an important task well done. The conviction that your mind or body is working at optimum speed or capacity. The utterly successful moment of love. Of such stuff are the great moments of pleasure made.

But because such experiences are common to us all, they do not singularize human beings. It is our minor pleasures that differentiate us, one from the other. In them the delicate lines of separation are drawn between individuals. And our wayward inclinations, our secret whims may, when totaled, be more revealing than our major experiences. When Charles Lamb remarked that his most gratifying pleasure was to do a good act by stealth and have it found out by accident, how much of himself was declared!

One of the deepest of minor pleasures is the common one of collecting. I say deep because it is rooted in the primitive. It is akin to the pleasure we take in being snug and warm when outside the elements are raging. It must respond to the caveman within. The philatelist will tell you that stamps are educational, that they are valuable, that they are beautiful. This is only part of the truth. My notion is that the collection is a hedge, a comfort, a shelter into which the sorely beset mind can withdraw. It is orderly, it grows toward completion, it is something that can't be taken away from us.

One of my unfailing minor pleasures may seem dull to more energetic souls: opening the mail. Living in an advanced industrial civilization, we have arranged things so that we know pretty much what's going to happen; the proper button is always there to be pressed. Such efficiency is admirable, but it does not afford scope to that perverse human trait, still not quite eliminated, which is pleased by the accidental. Thus to me the mail functions as the voice of the unpredictable and keeps alive for a few minutes a day the keen sense of the unplanned and the unplannable.

There are certain minor pleasures whose particular note is that of relief, such as the pleasure that comes of surviving a children's party for five-year-olds; or of the mildly illegitimate, such as the midnight raid on the refrigerator for the purpose of eating all the things that are bad for you; or of the unexpectedly comforting, such as awakening on a cold morning, consulting the clock and finding that you still have two hours of sleep; or of delay, such as the pleasure a writer feels in rearranging his desk, sharpening his pencils and lengthily informing each and every member of the family that, being about to set to work, he is not to be disturbed.

Whatever our pleasures may be, the important thing is never to fake them, never to attend a ball game because that is the right thing to do or read a book because it is fashionable. The discovery of what one really likes involves the discovery of oneself; it means having the courage not to imitate, not to conform. Bernard Shaw once warned us to be sure to get what we liked; otherwise we might begin to like what we got.

In our time of mass enjoyments it is all the more necessary for us to keep delving into the mysterious inner world of our selves, to isolate and develop our special pleasure skills.

CLIFTON FADIMAN

ONE MORE TIME

Just for a minute, Lord, let me be a child again. Not long ago, I knew those feelings, but they slipped away one day when I neglected to remember them. If I might just once again:

...Run as fast as I can for no reason but to feel the hard ground under my feet.

...Walk home from school kicking a rock and dragging a stick, amazed by tiny buds on the trees and the earth's awakening from winter's sleep.

...Press my nose against a rain-washed windowpane, reluctantly allowing the aroma of cookies baking in the kitchen to pull me from my watch.

...Stomp through puddles in spring's light rain until my pants and shoes are soaked. (Maybe there shouldn't be a punishment where there is no guilt.)

...Crouch behind a bush in the darkness during a game of hide-and-seek, heart pumping loudly, breath tight in my chest.

...Wobble down the sidewalk on my new bike, biting my lips in concentration as I ride alone for the first time.

...Lift my face, eyes squeezed shut and mouth open wide, to catch huge snowflakes on my tongue.

...Feel the tingling sleeplessness of Christmas Eve, listening for hoofs on the roof and really believing in Santa Claus, but almost knowing it isn't true.

When did I accept the difference between reality and make-believe? On what day did I start seeing with my mind instead of my heart?

I never planned to let these times escape when I moved into others. I didn't know they would hurry from me to become only fragrant reminders of a scent forgotten.

Please, Lord, let me be a child just one more time.

KATHRYN BACUS

SERENITY

TIME OUT FOR HAPPINESS

You can make your days richer if you polish up your happiness collection.

A few years ago I stopped in to see my cousin on a Saturday afternoon. She has five children and a busy schedule of community activities, but Saturdays, she had told me, were hobby days. Then each member of the family worked on special collections or some other personal interest.

When I arrived, her husband was refinishing an antique chair in the backyard. In the house, I admired one child's rock collection, another's hand–carved set of doll's furniture. Finally I reached the kitchen—and found my cousin sitting peacefully in a big armchair, looking out the window at the hills beyond her house. Surprised, I said I hoped she hadn't interrupted her hobbying on my account.

With a twinkle in her eye, she replied, "I'm working hard on my favorite hobby. Every Saturday afternoon, I polish up my happiness collection."

She explained that she loved this view, loved sitting in a comfortable chair with nothing to do, loved chatting or just dreaming. There was no time for these pleasures during her busy week. But on Saturdays she keeps her personal treasure in good order.

"Everyone has a happiness collection," she went on, "although many people fail to give it the importance it deserves. We tend to feel that small joys are trivial, foolish—perhaps because they are ours alone, and can't always be fully understood by someone else.''

I had not been aware of owning a happiness collection. But my cousin's words returned to me soon afterward. I had had a houseful of guests for five days. The morning after they left, I awoke to the realization that that day I need not entertain anyone, plan anything. My first impulse was to jump out of bed and catch up on neglected housework. Then I realized that I had an alternative: I could simply turn over and go back to sleep.

I did exactly that, then drank coffee and read a magazine for the rest of the morning, blissfully happy. Later I picked flowers, played with the dog, enjoyed myself. What a polishing my collection got that day! By nightfall, it glowed—and so did I. Next day, rested and refreshed, I caught up on the housework.

From this beginning, I learned to recognize countless bits of treasure that I had taken for granted before, or had even discarded as worthless. For example, when I was first married I loved to bake bread. There was something profoundly satisfying about kneading the dough, waiting for it to rise, taking the warm loaf from the oven. Yet almost every conceivable kind of loaf could be bought at less expense at a supermarket or at a bakery. So, merely because I could not justify bread-making except in terms of my own enjoyment, I got out of the habit of baking.

Now, cheered on by my wise cousin, I began again. How I relished going back over the old recipes, plunging elbow-high in flour! Ever since, the wonderful smell of my own bread baking has held an honored place in my happiness collection.

Often, of course, our lives seem too full of busyness for simple, private pleasures. But how hard do we really try to find the time? If we lost a valued piece of silver or broke a precious bit of china, we would berate ourselves for carelessness. Yet we throw away beloved small pleasures as though they had no value.

One evening, in a rare hour of recreation with friends, someone mentioned a story of a famous poet. On a visit to Italy, the poet had walked along a street with many beggars. One seemed to be attracting more attention — and more alms — than the others. The poet came near, and saw why. On a sign the man had written: "It is April and I am blind."

I saw my husband Russ's thoughtful expression. Next morning, he got up ten minutes earlier than usual and walked out into the garden where the flowers had burst open. I saw him pick a crocus and look into its small purple chalice. He brought it to the breakfast table. He said merely, "This is for the lady who shares spring with me." But his relaxed smile told me that he would not let the thief of busyness steal his treasures again.

In our house, we frequently remind each other to "take a happiness break," after which housework, homework, office work, seem easier. Best of all we're *happier*.

In Thornton Wilder's play *Our Town*, a young woman who has died is given the opportunity to relive one day of her life. Experiencing human existence for the second time, she sees how marvelous it is. When the time comes for her to leave forever, she says farewell to previous small miracles that she barely noticed when she was alive. In a touching scene, she brings home the truth that many seemingly humdrum aspects of everyday living can give us pleasure if we but take the time to contemplate them: the comforting ticking of a clock, the colors of flowers, the smell of new-brewed coffee, the relaxation of a hot bath, the coasting off to sleep when tired and the refreshed re-awakening.

We all have a second chance to appreciate life — while we live it, beginning right now.

ELIZABETH STARR HILL

HOW TO ENJOY THE HAPPIEST DAY
OF YOUR LIFE

We can do anything for one day. So, just for today, let us be unafraid of life, unafraid of death which is the shadow of life; unafraid to be happy, to enjoy the beautiful, to believe the best.

Just for today let us live one day only, forgetting yesterday and tomorrow, and not trying to solve the whole problem of life at once. Lincoln said that a man is just as happy as he makes up his mind to be. Suppose we make up our mind to be happy just for today, to adjust ourselves to what is — our family, our business, our luck. To try to make the world over to suit us is a large order. If we cannot have what we like, maybe we can like what we have.

So, just for today, let us be agreeable, responsive, cheerful, charitable; be our best, dress our best, walk softly, praise people for what they do, not criticize them for what they cannot do. And if we find fault, let us forgive it and forget.

JOSEPH FORT NEWTON

PRESCRIPTIONS FOR PEACE OF MIND

To start each day is to move into a troubled world. Yet somehow there has to be a way to begin afresh. Here is how four prominent Americans have managed to do it.

James Michener, noted author: I have two dogs — a big black German shepherd, and a smaller white hunting dog. I work rather hard, and the dogs accept this, stopping by my typewriter now and then to check on my progress. They have learned that never in the morning will I pay much attention to them because I'm a morning worker.

But come late afternoon, the dogs refuse to let me alone. They will come and sit by me, watch reproachfully, nip and growl at my ankles, until I leave whatever I am doing and go for a red jacket and a walking stick. Then they know the day is about to begin.

The three of us set out across fields, over fallen trees, along old streams and onto cleared land that has not been plowed for half a century. They are marvelous animals, true to their instincts, and when we are out, they want to roam, to sniff and to follow the trails they've discovered. They want very little interruption from me, and most of the time they are a good quarter of a mile away, for they have their own problems and I am not part of them.

And so we go for a couple of miles, and after we are all pretty tired we come home. Since the workday has been ruined by the interruption, there's no point in going back to the typewriter; so I sit in the living room as dusk falls and play Beethoven or the Beatles or opera selections, while the dogs rest.

I don't know what price I would place upon these two great animals. Let's say half my income, because they insist that I go out regularly to see the nature of which I am a part. I am lured by them into winter and summer, into the vast geological history of the land I live on, and along trails I would not otherwise have known.

More especially, they remind me that I, too, am an animal first and a thinking human being later. And I have come to believe that any living thing is better off when it lives closest to its inherent nature. I owe these two wonderful mutts a debt that could never be repaid, for they have taught me about myself and my world. It is in this way that I achieve whatever peace of mind I attain in this nutty world.

Michael E. DeBakey, heart-surgery pioneer, chancellor and chairman, Dept. of Surgery, Baylor College of Medicine: Because my working day is marked by pressures, emergencies, and demands of all kinds, I cherish the early morning hours when I can be alone and engage in a kind of self–communication. I arise at 4:30 a.m. every day and go to my study, where I can plan certain of my activities that require quiet meditation. The solitude of the early morning is the most precious time of my day—and the only time that I have totally to myself. For me, those early hours symbolize a rebirth; the anxieties, frustrations, and stresses of the preceding day seem to have been washed away during the night. God has granted another day of life—another chance to do something worthwhile for humanity.

Hugh Downs, for nine years host of NBC's TV show "Today": When I was younger, having been told, "Time is the stuff life is made of; do not squander it," I thought I ought to fill every moment with "meaningful" activity. This led to a sense of guilt about goofing off for an hour or a day. Fortunately, I have outgrown this. I now allow what I call my sense of responsibility to atrophy somewhat. If it is necessary for me to squander and waste some of my time in order to avoid derailment, then that time is not squandered or wasted.

We inherited an inordinate fondness for logic from the classic Greeks and put such emphasis on the rational that we are surprised when the intuitive side of our lives brings the things we want. So, in idle moments, I walk in the desert or tend plants in the tiny oasis I've created around my home. Or read or sleep or climb rocks. I don't try to think about anything or solve problems.

There is, of course, satisfaction in driving toward the solution of problems. But with me the effectiveness of such efforts is enhanced by the random, purposeless activity I now indulge in without guilt.

Terence Cardinal Cooke of New York: I like to meet people. I enjoy their company. Fortunately, both at home and overseas, I have the opportunity of meeting a great many people. It is true that I meet most of them only briefly, and often do not have the chance for a lengthy conversation. Still, it is surprising how much a person will tell in a few seconds about himself and the things that really concern him.

Now what has this got to do with "getting away from it all," retaining peace of mind, managing stress and pressure? Just this—I find the way to do all this with people.

When I am speaking face-to-face and heart-to-heart with another person, I don't feel pressure. Perhaps it is because in this setting I feel that I as a person can really do something for my brother. The person I speak with expects that I can put things in perspective because he takes for granted that I am a man of prayer and reflection. I am sure that every minister, priest and rabbi has this experience. And I find that being constantly thought of as a man of prayer helps me more and more to *be* a man of prayer. And there is no better way to make our pressures bearable than by taking ourselves and our problems to our Heavenly Father.

To sum up: "people and prayer"—one quite personal formula for peace of mind.

MANAGING STRESS

These simple techniques will help you to deal effectively with the many pressures of everyday living.

Betty Nelson* stood at the door of her 12-year-old's room, staring at the tangle of clothes, catcher's mitts and comic books. She felt her head begin to throb.

"Clean up this room, Billy," she snapped.

"No," he replied defiantly.

"That's the last straw!" she shrieked. "You're not going to baseball practice until this room is spotless." She slammed the door and stamped down the hall. The throb had turned into a stabbing pain behind her eyes.

Bob Nelson twisted a paper clip into lopsided loops while his boss pounded his fist on top of Bob's sales report and said, "You're slipping, Bob. Maybe you're getting too old to handle this territory." Bob felt his stomach churning as he left the

*The family name has been disguised.

office. He had worked hard to keep up sales but rising prices were a problem.

The Nelsons were experiencing stress, a physiological response to the pressures of daily living. Yet stress is vital to effective living.

Donald A. Tubesing, an educational psychologist, president of the Whole Person Associates in Duluth, Minn., and author of *Kicking Your Stress Habits* (Whole Person Associates, 1981), likens stress to the tension on a violin string. If the string is too taut, it snaps; but if it's too slack, it won't make music. In counseling hundreds of people like the Nelsons, he has developed a simple system for creative management of stress.

The first step is to determine whether you are experiencing useful or destructive stress. Ask yourself these questions: Do little things irritate me? Do I have trouble sleeping, and wake up tired and grouchy? Do I worry a lot? Feel trapped? Complain? Frequently snap at those I love? Do I suffer physical symptoms?

If you answered "yes" to even one question, you may be experiencing harmful stress.

There are many stressors—sources of stress—such as internal or external pressure to succeed, success itself, conflicts with children or mates, unrealistic expectations, too many people to please, too little sleep, money worries, lack of self-confidence, a conflict in values, lack of goals. Things which stress one person may not stress another, and things which cause stress at one point in a person's life may not at another point.

A stressor is neutral, says Tubesing. Our reactions to it—based on personal beliefs and values—are what give it positive or negative power over our lives.

Imagine waking up and glancing at your clock, which reads 8:55 a.m. This information means nothing, until you apply your perception to it. If it's a weekday, you're due at work at 9 a.m., and being punctual is important, 8:55 becomes a negative stressor. If it's Saturday, your perception of 8:55 may result in a feeling of luxurious anticipation of a lazy day. The information in both cases was the same. Your perception of it determined your response.

Tubesing asks participants in the Stress Skills Workshops he and his associates conduct throughout the country to fill in the blanks in the following statements.

- Maybe I don't need to _____ anymore.
- Maybe I do need to _____ some more _____.
- Maybe I need to _____ sometime soon.
- Maybe I need to _____ once again.
- Maybe I need to _____ sometimes.

The first statement clarifies what you would like to change; the second what you want to hang on to. The third is a statement of future goals, while the fourth recalls a resource from the past. The fifth clarifies an area where you need more flexibility.

"Many people feel trapped. They see no alternatives," says Tubesing. "They must learn that they do have choices, and that they create their own world by the choices they make." Often stress reactions are simply the result of habitual responses to certain circumstances, Tubesing points out. But we can break those stress habits over a period of time by consciously making different choices. He offers four techniques for taking charge of your reactions to stressors:

Reorganize yourself. Take control of the way you spend your time; learn to avoid using $10 worth of energy on a 10-cent problem. Tubesing suggests that you use the results of his fill-in-the-blank statements to isolate goals, and then draw up a plan—for the next five years, year, month and day—listing specific actions to achieve those goals.

Change the scene. Bob decided to try managing his stress by using Tubesing's second technique, controlling his environment with the aid of scene-changing skills. These include fight, flight (which Tubesing says is positive, not negative—the art of retreat to find or create another setting more conducive to your inner peace) and listening. At work, Bob chose flight, leaving his stress-producing job to open his own business, where he could use his accumulated know-how and contacts but answer only to himself. At home, he tried listening, "the art of tuning in to the feelings of others."

Change your mind. You can manage stress by taking control of your attitude, too, particularly through techniques Tubesing describes as relabeling, whispering and imagination. Relabeling, "the art of seeing a promise in every problem," allowed Betty to relax when Billy challenged her authority. Instead of seeing his rebellion as a lack of respect for her, she learned to see it as a sign of his growing independence.

Whispering, "the art of giving yourself positive messages when things are going wrong," was a mind-changing skill Bob and Betty found difficult at first. "We all talk to ourselves about ourselves," says Tubesing, "so why not talk nicely?" He taught Betty to whisper, "I am a good wife and mother" whenever she felt uptight about her house, husband or son.

Imagination, "the art of laughter," is the ability to accept and appreciate the incongruities of life. "If you can laugh at yourself," says Tubesing, "it sets you apart from your problem. Then you can tackle it from a new perspective."

Build up your strength. Another way of managing stress is to build up your stamina. Tubesing urged Bob and Betty to eat a healthful diet, to arrange daily relaxation times, and to get in the habit of exercising.

All of us have resources which we use to cope with stress. However, if we are feeling physical symptoms of stress, our regular resources or "energizers" clearly aren't doing the job, so we need to develop new ones. To help identify your resources, which can be people, settings or activities, Tubesing offers his personal list:

Physical resources: jogging, pruning the shrubs. Emotional: hugging my kids, paying my wife a compliment. Social: phoning a friend, having a party. Intellectual: reading, listening to music. Spiritual: admiring the beauty of the world around me, spending ten minutes meditating.

The key to choosing an effective energizer is that it must give you a new perspective on your life. If you usually turn to physical exercise when you feel stressed, try doing a crossword puzzle. If you normally watch television, run around the block.

Through practice, you can break your stress habits by reacting differently to the pressures of daily living. Identify your stressors, find out how they are stressing you, develop a stockpile of energizers and use them to reorganize yourself, change the scene, change your mind and build up your strength. Over a period of time new, more healthful ways of coping with stress will replace your old, destructive ones.

JENNIFER BOLCH

10 THINGS I LEARNED IN A HALF CENTURY OF LIVING

1. A man who wants time to read and write must let the grass grow long.

2. The hardest part of raising children is teaching them to ride bicycles. A shaky child on a bicycle for the first time needs both support and freedom. The realization that this is what the child will always need can hit hard.

3. It's impossible to treat a child too well. Children are spoiled by being ignored too much or by harshness, not by kindness. Rich kids are often spoiled not by their toys and automobiles, but by parents who are too busy to pay much attention to them.

4. It is impossible to treat a woman too well.

5. The definition of a beautiful woman is one who loves me.

6. Children go away and live their own lives, starting when they are about 18. Parents who accept this as a natural part of the order of things will see their grown children surprisingly often.

7. Success in almost any field depends more on energy and drive than it does on intelligence.

8. When things break around the house, call a handyman. No intelligent man is capable of fixing anything, unless he has made home repair his business.

9. Either afloat or ashore, it is normal for everything to go wrong. No one should ever be surprised or unduly upset by foul-ups. They are a basic part of the human condition.

10. When I was young I was briefly interested in politics, but politics soon bored me. I was interested in business for a long while, but business eventually bored me. Although it may sound sentimental, the only real meaning I have found in life has been in my wife and children. Without them, I would be in more despair than a bankrupt millionaire.

SLOAN WILSON

SHARING

HOW TO GET AWAY FROM YOURSELF

Bored? Tired? Fed-up? Maybe you are suffering from an all-too-common malady: self-centeredness. Here are some suggestions for a cure...

"There was a young lady of Guelph,
Who was wholly wrapped up in herself;
    It would have been kinder,
    To try to unwind her,
But they left her in knots on the shelf."

This limerick points to an all-too-common human malady. Being wrapped up in oneself is back of a good deal of despondency—that "drained feeling," as though all the zest had gone out of living. The remedy, of course, is to "get away from yourself." But how do you do that?

"Isolation is a frequent factor in mental and emotional disturbances," said the late Dr. Maurice Greenhill, then director of the New York City Community Mental Health Board. "When we tell someone to 'get away from himself,' we are simply asking him to break that isolation, to reach out and make contact with other people."

Here is an easy way to begin: write a letter. Perhaps there is a relative with whom you haven't been in touch for a long time, or a friend who has moved to another town. By writing to that fellow human you reach outside yourself.

One man who had been depressed for months finally broke away by what he called the "talk-to-someone plan."

"Starting one Monday morning, I made it my business to

talk with someone new every day of the week," he said. "Monday it was the elevator starter at the office, to whom I had hardly spoken three words before. Tuesday I went into the office across the hall and had a wonderful chat with a man whom I had never really known though he had been my neighbor for seven years. Wednesday it was a man waiting in line with me where I eat lunch; Thursday, the news dealer; Friday, the drugstore man. Now I never let a day go by without 'breaking the ice' with someone new."

This man's era of isolation—and his depression—were over.

"No tree bears fruit for its own use," said Martin Luther. "Everything in God's will gives itself."

You get away from yourself by giving *of yourself.* A woman went to the Red Cross chapter in her city. She had been sinking deeper and deeper into the blues, and a friend had suggested that she do some charity work in her spare time. "Let me be frank about this," she told the girl at the desk. "I'm offering to help wherever I can. But it's mainly to help *myself* that I'm offering to help *you.*"

Actually she did a good job for both.

There is inertia in human emotions, a tendency to stay in a path or pattern unless some *force* is applied to change the direction. Dr. Robert H. Felix, former director of the National Institute of Mental Health, says, "If you commune only with yourself, you simply go around in circles. If you feel abused and put upon, neglected and unloved, and you stay in your own little shell, you simply feel more abused and put upon, more neglected and unloved."

Break this vicious circle by action, Dr. Felix suggests. What action? Choose from your own hobbies, skills and pastimes. Go on a hike with friends, build a lamp in your workshop, get out the gardening tools—don't just sit there!

"Activity itself does the trick," says Dr. Felix. And activity is possible even if one is immobilized. A 79-year-old woman, confined to a wheel chair after an automobile accident, faced a dull and lonely future. One day she rolled herself down to the newsstand near her home and chatted with the crippled veteran who operated it. She learned he couldn't have a hot lunch because he had no helper. At 86 she was still doing a daily stint —tending the stand for him. "Instead of being alone, I am making many new friends," she said.

For people who are essentially well, suffering only from the minor cuts and bruises of emotional life and not from the grave maladies, self-help is possible. At one psychiatric clinic a patient who complained of excessive fatigue was told, "When you're tired, go to work." Strange advice? Not in this case, which, like so many, was a case of emotional fatigue.

A doctor at the clinic remarked, "You'd be amazed how people suffering from emotional fatigue won't admit it. They want to blame it on secondary anemia or low blood pressure— but never on just plain boredom. Even after we've checked out all possible physical causes, they'd rather have a pill or a medicine than face the task of getting interested in someone or something outside themselves."

Religion always has stressed the need to break through the prison of the self. Years ago I attended a religious retreat conducted by the missionary-evangelist E. Stanley Jones. The purpose of the week-long meeting was, as Dr. Jones put it, "to get people out of themselves."

"Self-centeredness," he remarked, "is the cause of one of our most common allergies. People are allergic to themselves." The cure, as he prescribed it: work, sharing with others, surrender of self to God.

A businessman who had been remarkably successful, but couldn't sleep nights, said at the week's end: "Up to now I've been too proud to seek help. Now I feel relieved and peaceful inside because for once in my life I've gotten down on my knees and admitted I didn't have all the answers."

The man had learned to pray. Help had been there all the time, but that alone wasn't enough. He now was willing to receive it. "Prayer," it has been said, "is not overcoming God's reluctance. It is taking hold of God's willingness."

There is also the willingness of one's fellow man. The individual imprisoned in himself often sees the rest of the world as hostile. He keeps other people at arm's length. Such a person can never feel the warmth of meaningful association, the quality in another human being which reaches out to touch him in fellowship.

If the person who is withdrawn because of extreme shyness will make himself reachable by reaching out toward others, he may be in for a surprise. Other people will seem to have changed. They won't seem to be shutting him out at all.

Strange, isn't it — all that change in *others*, when the only real change has been in oneself!

HOWARD WHITMAN

The difference between the word "sharing" and the word "charity" is far greater than semantic. The charitable person merely listens to his own music; the sharing person participates in a symphony, mingling his notes with those of others, caught up in the intoxicating excitement of creating a grand crescendo in unison.

JACQUES COUSTEAU

THE ART OF PAYING A COMPLIMENT

One of the best ways to smooth relations with other people is to be adept at the art of paying a compliment. The sincere, appreciative remark helps the other fellow to realize his own inherent worth. And, what is more, the ability to pay a compliment bolsters our own ego — which is not a bad thing either.

We never forget a compliment that has deeply pleased us, nor do we forget the person who made it. Like all ventures in human relations, the art of paying a compliment takes thought and practice. We have all experienced the remorse of having our praise fall flat because we chose the wrong time to give it or the wrong language to couch it in.

According to Leonard Lyons, a compliment of the right sort was paid Toscanini by Judith Anderson when she saw him after a concert.

"She didn't say I had conducted well," said the maestro. "I knew that. She said I looked handsome." It is human nature to enjoy praise for something we are not noted for. When someone calls attention to an unadvertised facet of our personality it makes him forever our friend.

We all pride ourselves on our individual distinctions. It is a gross misconception to think you are complimenting a person by telling him he looks exactly like so-and-so, even if so-and-so is a movie idol. I have noticed that nothing pleases us less than to have a double.

One of the most satisfying kinds of compliment to give or receive is the double, or relayed, compliment — one passed on to you by someone who heard it. Recently, a correspondent enclosed a letter he had received from a friend who happens to be a man of eminence in his field. This man's opinion of a column I had written puffed me up considerably. Relayed to me by my friend, it was a compliment amplified — far more effective than if it had come direct.

The ingenuous compliment may touch us deeply, but it is probably the hardest to pay, for it depends on pure inspiration. I am reminded of an example that Margery Wilson cites in her book *Make Up Your Mind*. She once had a butler who knew a great deal about sculpture. His hero was Gutzon Borglum, the man who carved the massive portraits of Washington, Jefferson, Lincoln and Theodore Roosevelt on a mountainside in the Black Hills of South Dakota. Borglum came to tea and the butler, beside himself with excitement, spilled a glass of wine on him. Swabbing the sculptor desperately with a napkin, the butler said, "I could have served a lesser man perfectly."

To his embarrassed worshiper Borglum replied, "I was never so complimented in my life!"

Among the varieties of compliment is one with a particularly pleasing punch; I should call it a "bonus compliment of recall." It is indeed a heart-warming surprise when a person remembers something you said a long time ago that made a lasting impression on him. That it should have been hoarded and served up to you at an appropriate time is an experience bound to smooth out your kinks of self-doubt.

Urging me to go on a trip, a friend once said, "Memories are the best investment you can make." It was just as casual as that, yet it gave me courage to travel as I might not have, thinking I ought not to invest the money or the time. When I later reminded my friend of his remark, I found he had completely forgotten the incident. But my reminding him nourished his ego anew.

Compliments offered in the kidding vein hit home just as surely as those with a serious-minded approach. And they involve no responsibility on the part of the receiver for a rejoinder. He can laugh with the crowd and happily accept his accolade.

I overheard a remark of this type in a restaurant recently. A group of businessmen were finishing lunch at the table next to mine. Said one of them, "Harry is the best computing machine here; he's a real mathemagician. So he gets stuck with figuring out the check!" They all chuckled; it was obviously a compliment.

Pushed to the point of flattery, the compliment is distasteful to most of us. We have all known people so vain that no syrup is too sweet for their taste, but they are in the minority. If we have any sense of proportion about ourselves, we are at once aware that we are being overpraised. This can be as painful as criticism.

Sometimes in a group of people we get so caught up in our own good words for a person that we overplay a tribute. When we finally stop, the recipient feels called upon to fill the sudden void in conversation with refutation equal in violence.

A compliment casually worked in, so that the threads of general conversation can easily be retrieved, makes less demands on the recipient — and leaves him with more glow than he would have gained from the spotlight. For example, as simple a thing as a question may become a compliment. If, instead of telling Bill that you think he has a wonderful garden, you ask him for advice about yours, you accomplish a number of things. You have indicated that you admire his gardening skill: you have singled him out from the crowd. He can give you advice without any to-do about acknowledging the compliment. And he's likely to feel you are a discerning guy.

When a man by virtue of success comes in for constant personal kudos, we face a dilemma when we want to get across to him our feelings of admiration. We know he must be tired of hearing the same things, of making the same perfunctory acknowledgment. Here is a place where we can use the indirect compliment to great advantage by telling him how much we admire his children, his house, his garden, a picture that hangs in his living room. In effect we are telling him that we admire what he admires. A man may question the truth of what we say about *him*, but he will not question a tribute to the things he loves.

One of the choicest indirect compliments I have heard was a husband's anniversary greeting to his wife: "I love you not only for what you are, but for what I am when I am with you." She prized those words more than the handsome present.

Compliments smooth the paths of social intercourse, help to dispel the recurrent dissatisfaction most of us have with ourselves and encourage us toward new achievement. "Appreciative words," says Dr. George W. Crane, "are the most powerful force for good will on earth."

J. DONALD ADAMS

SEND SOMEONE A SMILE

It's simple. It takes only a moment. And, as this young mother discovered, it can lift your own spirits.

One day shortly after my third child was born, I received a note from another young mother, a friend of mine who lived just three blocks from me. We hadn't seen each other all winter. "Hi, friend," she wrote. "I think of you often. Someday we'll have time to spend together like in the old days. Keep plugging. I know you're a super mother. See you soon, I hope." It was signed: "Your friend on hold, Sue Ann."

The few words lifted my spirits and added a soothing ointment of love to a hectic day. I remember thinking, *Thanks, Sue Ann. I needed that.*

The next day was my errand day, because my husband was home to tend the children. I decided to visit a card shop a few miles away that was having a sale. I wasn't in a good mood. The baby had a cold, and I was in a hurry.

Instead of reacting to my brusqueness, the saleswoman was extremely courteous and helpful. Noticing that her name tag read Janet Sullivan, I asked the woman if she was the store owner. "Oh, no," she said. "I'm just one of the employees, but I love it here." I left the shop feeling more able to cope.

On the way home, I thought, *I really ought to write a note to the owner of that shop and tell her what a good employee Janet Sullivan is. But, of course, there isn't time.*

When I arrived home, however, things seemed peaceful. On my desk I saw my friend Sue Ann's note. If she had the time to lift my spirits, why, I had time to help cheer others.

"Dear Store Owner," I wrote. "It was a hectic morning and I came into your shop with a chip on my shoulder. But Janet Sullivan was pleasant, extremely helpful, and she did not let my uptight mood affect her kindness to me. Thank you for hiring such a lovely lady and for making my day better." I signed the note "A satisfied customer."

Next I wrote to Janet Sullivan. It all took only a few minutes, but the rest of my day seemed to glide by more smoothly than usual. I decided I would write notes more often when I ran into people who were doing a good job.

That Monday my six-year-old came home from school with a clever puppet and several other delightful learning tools. For quite a while, I had been impressed with the good job Meagan's teacher was doing, yet I had never told her.

Why not? I thought, as I pulled out another sheet of stationery.

I decided not to sign the note. I didn't want Miss Patrick to think I was trying to help my daughter to be better-liked.

When I went out to mail Miss Patrick's note, I noticed a neighbor checking his mailbox. Mr. Williams' head drooped and his pace seemed slower as he shuffled back to his house empty-handed. I hurried back into my own house because I could hear my baby crying, but I couldn't get Mr. Williams off my mind. It wasn't a check he was waiting for; he was quite well-to-do. He was probably looking for some love in his mailbox.

While Meagan drew a picture of a mailbox with a smile in it and Tami drew a rainbow, I wrote a little note. "We are your secret admirers," it began. We added a favorite story and a poem. "Expect to hear from us often," I wrote on the envelope.

The next day my children and I watched Mr. Williams take out his mail and open the envelope right in the driveway. Even at a distance, we could see he was smiling.

My mind began reeling when I thought of all the people who could use smiles in their mailboxes. Even on busy days I could find the time to write at least one note.

Hundreds of notes later, I have made two discoveries:

1. Notes don't need to be long. When my neighbors the Linthrops moved, I heard several other neighbors comment on how much they missed them. My note from our street was extremely short.

"Dear Linthrops," I wrote. "When you moved, you took some sunshine with you. People here miss your smiles and happy voices. Please come back to visit.

Your friend on Cherry Lane."

2. Anonymous notes leave others free of obligation. It is difficult for people to accept compliments or help, and anonymous notes alleviate any embarrassment or feelings that they must acknowledge or reciprocate in any way.

Perhaps I will never have the means and the time to help others in magnificent ways, even after our children are grown. But right now it is satisfying to know that I am helping to lift spirits in small ways. I have found that it is easy to find the time to write letters of praise, love and appreciation. And as a side effect, I find myself looking at my own circumstances in a much more positive light. But then happiness usually is a side effect.

ANN BATEMAN

Happiness is a perfume you cannot pour on others without getting a few drops on yourself.

EMERSON

FUN, OH BOY, FUN!

Suzanne Britt Jordan remembers a special gift from a friend—a day of fun she'll never forget.

Fun, a rare jewel, is hard to have.

Somewhere along the line, people got the modern idea that fun was there for the asking, that people deserved fun, that if we didn't have a little fun every day we would turn into (sakes alive!) puritans.

"Was it fun?" became the question that overshadowed all other questions, good questions like: Was it moral? Was it kind? Was it beneficial? Was it necessary? And (my favorite) was it selfless?

When pleasure got to be the main thing, the fun fetish was sure to follow. Everything was supposed to be fun. If it wasn't fun, then, by Jove, we were going to make it fun, or else.

Television commercials brought a lot of fun and fun-loving folks into the picture. Everything that people did in those commercials looked like fun: swilling beer, buying insurance, mopping the floor, taking aspirin. But the more commercials we watched, the more we wondered when the fun would start in our own lives. It was pretty depressing.

It occurred to me, while I was sitting around waiting for the fun to start, that not much *is* fun, and that I should tell you just in case you're worried about your fun capacity.

I don't mean to put a damper on things. I just mean we ought to treat fun reverently. It is a mystery. It cannot be caught like a virus. It cannot be trapped like an animal. When it does come in, on little dancing feet, you probably won't be expecting it. In fact, I bet it comes when you're doing your duty or your work. It may even come on a Tuesday.

I remember one day, long ago, on which I had an especially good time. Pam Smith and I walked to the College Village drugstore one Saturday morning to buy some candy. We were about 12 years old (fun ages). She got her Bit-O-Honey, I got my Chunkys and M&M's. We started back to her house. I was going to spend the night. We had the whole day to look forward to. And we had plenty of candy.

It was a long way to Pam's house, but every time we got weary Pam would put her hand over her eyes, scan the horizon like a sailor and say, "Oughta reach home by nightfall," at which point the two of us would laugh until we thought we couldn't stand it. Then, after we got calm, she'd say it again.

You should have been there. It was the kind of day and friendship and occasion that made me regret that I ever had to grow up.

It was fun.

SUZANNE BRITT JORDAN

LET'S REALLY TALK

My wife recently invited a young couple over to our place. "You mean—just to talk?" the woman said, eyes wide in horror. "Let's go dancing!"

While we all hopped around like agitated protons, I wondered, *What's wrong with just talking? It's an honorable human activity, isn't it?*

Since then, I have been listening to Americans talk, and I am appalled. Lively conversation is a goner. Once Walt Whitman could exult, "I hear America singing." Today all we can muster is a somnolent mumble. Or a yakety-yak, which is to conversation what a hot dog is to *haute cuisine.*

TV is one culprit. I have heard sane adults argue that TV talk shows are reviving the art of conversation. Balderdash. Conversation isn't something you watch; it's something you do. People pitch in to build a good conversation the way they used to build a barn together or sew a patchwork quilt.

But TV is not solely to blame. We like to buy our entertainment already packaged. Driving home from a movie with friends one night, my wife asked, "What did you think of it?" The woman said, "Um." Her husband added, "Uh, it was okay." So much for that conversation!

If we don't "um," we "yak." We gabble about our kids' cutenesses, about what we are having for dinner, about the status of our sore knee. We're too busy talking to ourselves, about ourselves, to notice that everyone else in the room is snoozing.

In 1968, when the Vietnam war was raging, I was at a dinner. Somehow, I began to discuss the war with a stranger.

Our opinions were poles apart, and the discussion quickly escalated into a yelling argument. We trumpeted like elephants.

But my opponent was no two-dimensional phantasm on a TV newscast. He was a worried man with a draft-age son, whose possible butchering in an Asian jungle he could accept only if he believed the war was right. Never again could I automatically assume that people whose opinions I despise are despicable. Conversation makes us look at each other.

Of course, it is not all fireworks. When I was in high school, a few of us would walk miles along country roads at night, talking about everything from the Meaning of Life (a subject only adolescents can handle) to the wonders of Jayne Mansfield to Fords versus Chevys. We just enjoyed one another's company.

All of my life's high points, it seems, were good conversations. Suddenly the talk takes an unexpected turn and doors open for you. Maybe it's not the subject that makes a conversation click, but the verve. And maybe to start one, all we have to do is break through the "me barrier" — go spelunking in other people's thoughts.

The most charming conversation I have had in years was with an eight-year-old girl. We all were driving to a fair. And, typical of so many of us these days, we adults had little to say. It looked to be a dull journey.

"What's your favorite color?" the girl asked me.

That was a stumper. "Sunlight," I said finally.

"Hmm," she said. "That means you like swallows and swimming. My favorite color is orange. Guess why. Give up? Because pumpkins are orange and that means autumn, which means school starting again. Did you like school when you were a kid?"

It was a swell afternoon. There's hope.

RICHARD WOLKOMIR

FOUR PRICELESS GIFTS FOR THOSE YOU LOVE

In a psychological study, children were asked what they liked about grandparents. Young children liked grandparents who gave them material things. But by the time kids were eight or nine, they preferred grandparents who would become mutually involved in activities — who gave them the gift of fun.

Already these children sensed something we adults too often forget in our thing-oriented culture: Toys can be terrific, and opals sparkle for many years. But usually the delight that comes from a material gift is brief, while a psychological gift can be a source of continuous joy and improved emotional health. Here are four important emotional gifts that we can give.

Boosting Self-Esteem. As a psychologist, I know that one of the most fundamental human needs is to feel good about oneself. People with healthy self-esteem can take things in their stride. They can meet other people without excessive shyness, feel comfortable in almost any social interaction, leave themselves open to change, and deal flexibly and soundly with most situations. They listen to others, but when they have to make a decision they tend to rely on their own inner counsel.

One of the best ways to get a sense of self-esteem is as a gift from other people. We can help others, for example, when we recognize their success at a task. Even young children like to be complimented for a job well done.

Letting Fun In. Unfortunately we all know people who destroy self-esteem. They can find the flaw in the most perfect situation.

How much better if we can fortify ourselves and our loved ones with humor. Like a suit of armor, the capacity to laugh at ourselves and at the absurdity of a situation can serve to protect us.

Wise, courageous people know how to give the gift of

humor to those they love!

Giving Up a Bad Habit. Have you ever thought what a wonderful gift it would be, not only for you but for those you love, if you could change an unhealthful or unhappy habit?

A first step in giving up a habit is to increase your motivation.

There are some ways you can do this. For example, list the reasons why you should change the habit. Also, list the "pay-offs" you may be getting unconsciously from the habit.

A second step is to keep a day-by-day record, noting each instance of the behavior you want to change. Take a long, hard look at the triggers setting off that behavior.

Then learn to substitute. I try to help people think of what habit they will *take* up, rather than *give* up.

Disclosing Ourselves. "Playing it cool" is a popular American game. It's based on the notion that if others know something about you they will use that knowledge to harm you. This is fine when you're playing cards. In the human-relationships game, however, poker-faced, non-disclosing people are big losers.

People who open up usually have more friends than people who don't. When you don't "let it out," there's no space for anyone to come in.

It's important, too, to let those we love know if we are feeling "high" or "low."

Each time we conceal something from someone close to us, the relationship becomes a little poorer. True, self-disclosure isn't always easy. But when we can't be honest with others, we can't be honest with ourselves. If we can remain authentic, we can give those around us some wonderful gifts. We can say, with Walt Whitman:

"Behold, I do not give lectures or a little charity,
"When I give I give myself."

DANIEL A. SUGARMAN

STARTING A HEALTHIER, HAPPIER LIFE

HOW HAPPY ARE YOU?

Most of us know when we're unhappy, and we're often aware of fleeting joyous moments. But the question "How happy are you?" can be difficult to answer. Based on traits found to be common among happy, well-adjusted people, this quiz can help you assess your happiness.

Choose the response to each question closest to your own feeling or situation. If none of the responses seems quite right, you may check two, but no more.

1. Given your pick of the following jobs, which would you choose?

a. A difficult, challenging assignment. If you can bring this off, you'll be promoted to an executive job. *b.* A job you can excel in because it's ideally suited to your energies and talents. *c.* A fairly modest job that involves working closely with a very powerful, important person.

2. Do you enjoy doing favors?

a. Yes. I seldom refuse when asked. *b.* Yes, when it's convenient and will really *help* someone. *c.* Not really. But I oblige when I feel I owe it to the person or if there's some compelling reason.

3. Which description best fits your usual sleeping pattern?

a. Sound sleeper, little trouble falling asleep. *b.* Light sleeper, easily awakened. *c.* Sound sleeper, difficulty falling asleep.

4. Are there occasions when you need to be alone?

a. Absolutely. *b.* No. I love having people around. *c.* No. I don't mind being alone, but wouldn't say I have a need for it.

5. How important do you feel it is to keep your surroundings neat and orderly?

a. Very important. I can put up with sloppiness in others, but never in myself. *b.* Important. In fact, I wish I were more orderly. *c.* Fairly important. I'm rather neat and don't care much for mess or squalor. *d.* Unimportant. I'd rather be in a messy house where people are relaxed than in a tidy one where everybody's fussy and uptight.

6. Which of the following would you be least *likely to want for a friend? The person who is...*

a. Snobbish and pretentious. *b.* A bully, cruel to those who can't fight back. *c.* Crude, pushy, ill-mannered.

7. In the past six months, how many times have you stayed home because of illness?

a. None. *b.* One. *c.* Two or more.

8. Something distressing has happened to a loved one — the death of someone close, perhaps. Your reaction?

a. I'd try to console him and cheer him up. *b.* I'd be as upset as he was — when he hurts, I hurt, too. *c.* I'd let him know I am sorry, but would continue to treat him the way I normally do.

9. How punctual are you?

a. Extremely punctual. I have an exact time sense. *b.* Quite *un*punctual. *c.* It varies. *d.* Quite punctual. I usually arrive when I'm supposed to.

10. How long do you remain angry with someone who has been unfair to you?

a. A long time. I don't easily forgive bad treatment. *b.* I wouldn't get angry. Anger is the product of a troubled mind. *c.* Not long. I get angry, but seldom hold a grudge. *d.* I don't stay angry, but will usually avoid the person from then on.

11. You inherit several million dollars. How would you

react?

a. I'd be delighted! *b.* I'd anticipate problems, but accept the money anyway. *c.* I'd be very worried about handling such a huge sum—it would mean starting a whole new life.

12. What would you find most appealing in a marriage partner?

a. Good-looking. *b.* Rich. *c.* Intelligent. *d.* Compatible. *e.* A terrific lover. *f.* Understanding.

13. Which statement best describes your social style?

a. I tend to keep to a small circle of close friends. *b.* I'm active socially and know hundreds of people. *c.* I have a lot of friends but don't stay in touch with them. I usually associate with whoever comes to see me.

14. With which of the following would you agree?

a. Time passes quickly, almost in a blur. *b.* Time moves slowly. *c.* Days are long, but weeks and months speed by. *d.* Days seem fast, weeks and months slow.

15. How do you feel about your present situation—personal qualities, friends and family, career, prospects for the future?

a. Wonderful! And the future looks bright. *b.* Pretty good. My situation may not be marvelous, but it's okay, and improving steadily. *c.* Fair. But I'm striving for a much better future. *d.* My feelings vary. Sometimes I feel good about myself, sometimes not.

Answers to "How Happy Are You?" Quiz

Check your answers against the list below. Give yourself one point for each correct ("happy") answer.

1. b	4. c	7. a or b	10. c	13. c
2. b	5. c	8. c	11. a	14. d
3. a	6. b	9. d	12. d	15. b

If you got two points or fewer, there isn't, unfortunately, much joy in your life. Four is better and six very good — you experience many happy moments. Seven points or more qualifies you as a happy person. Following is a description of each trait, along with the number or numbers of the questions where "right" answers suggest you possess these happy qualities.

The happy person likes to do useful, productive work, to use his abilities fully (1). He enjoys helping people, but is not self-sacrificing (2). At night, sleep researchers have found, he has little trouble falling asleep (3). He tends to be self-sufficient and can enjoy both solitude and company but is dependent on neither (4, 13). Generally, he's orderly and punctual (5, 9).

Though tolerant of people's minor flaws, the happy person dislikes cruelty and destructiveness (6). He is healthy (7), has no hang-ups about prosperity (11), and refuses to participate in other people's negative emotions (8) — or cling to his own (10). When choosing a mate, he will pick a congenial, compatible figure rather than someone romantic and glamorous (12). Like many busy, absorbed people, he feels days pass quickly, though in larger units — weeks, months, years — time may seem endless (14). Finally, the happy person has a sense of progress, improvement, of getting somewhere (15).

ROBERT HARRINGTON

FEELING FINE

Seven simple tips on how to enjoy a healthier, happier life.

Do you want to feel fine? Then forget about *absolute* self-control. Forget *complete* relaxation. Forget the promises of *total* fitness. Few of us are capable of such ideal states. But all of us have the capacity to *feel fine* — to live happily in a stressful world without being overwhelmed — if we will only take charge of our lives and become involved in a program of self-care.

That doesn't mean life should be a matter of constant self-denial. In fact, the full enjoyment of life is the best prescription I know for staying healthy. To feel fine, you have to know what your feelings and desires are and pay attention to them. Of course, you can't neglect diet or physical fitness; they're both part of feeling fine. But just as important are emotional and mental health, the keys to our total well-being. Here are seven suggestions for making you healthier and happier. Remember: Don't just read them, *do* them.

1. Break a taboo. Did you ever want to read a book in bed all night, but found yourself turning out the lights at the regular hour? Have you ever wanted steak for breakfast, but wound up eating eggs again?

You can break out of inhibiting habits if you make a list of some of the things you've never done but would like to do. They may be small things like those mentioned above. Or big things — like talking to strangers, or doing something you avoided in the past because men or women simply "don't do" such things.

Today or tomorrow, deliberately break a taboo or two.

2. Wake up your senses. How often do you touch — without feeling? Eat — without tasting? Breathe — without smelling? Look — without seeing? Listen — without hearing? Most of the time your senses are asleep. You turn them off so they won't distract you from the tasks you are doing.

Start to awaken your body to the pleasures that lie within. Cut a piece of fruit or a fresh vegetable into slices. How does it taste? Look closely at a familiar surface — a door, a leaf, the back of your hand. How many things are there that you never noticed? Close your eyes and count how many different sounds you can hear in three minutes. Take a half-dozen jars from your spice shelf. Close your eyes and smell each one separately. How long does it take you to distinguish among them without reading the labels? Gently massage your temples. Which spot provides the most relaxation? These are only a few of the opportunities waiting to stroke your senses — if you let them.

3. Show appreciation. Not long ago a valued friend told me how discouraged some of my staff members were because they were putting out their best for me, but my attitude seemed to show that I didn't care. "Of course I care," I answered.

"Then the solution is simple," he replied. "Let them know."

In the past, when my children finished practicing their music, I always asked why they didn't spend more time at it. Now I try to tell them how good they sounded. And instead of just increasing my tip when I get excellent service in a restaurant, I leave a few kind words, too.

A funny thing is happening. I'm noticing more nice things in my life. People are more fun to be around. Or maybe *I'm* more fun to be around.

4. Spend a buck. How often have you decided that a small, spur-of-the-moment gift that you knew a friend would enjoy wasn't good enough to give — because it cost only a dollar? Or not spent a buck on yourself because the purchase wasn't something you really needed? Try seeing how much pleasure you can squeeze out of a dollar — or two if you really feel high-spirited. Treat someone to a cup of coffee. Buy a flower and give it away. Give a dollar away, as a present to yourself.

5. *Enjoy your treasures.* Fifteen years ago I bought three bottles of a much-acclaimed champagne. I couldn't afford them at the time, but the shopkeeper assured me I'd never get another chance to buy champagne like that. For 15 years I kept those bottles, just waiting for an occasion big enough to pop the cork. Then someone told me that champagne can spoil if kept too long. That night, with no occasion at all to celebrate, my wife and I opened the bottles one by one. Of the three, two were undrinkable and the third was just so-so. It was a hard way to learn that the treasures of life have no value if they go unused.

Find a treasure you've been hoarding, and use it. Serve dinner to the kids on your best china. Pour the milk into crystal glasses. Put candles on the table. Use the "company" linen. Display those family heirlooms that are locked away in a closet. Break out the champagne!

6. *Trust your feelings.* *"Deux cents francs,"* the artist said. "Forty-five dollars." My heart pounded as I looked at his work. It was no Van Gogh, but there on an easel in Montmartre was a painting that captured all of my feelings about Paris. Still, my practical side told me that $45 was too much to pay for it. "Thirty-five dollars," I whispered. *"Deux cents francs,"* repeated the artist, and his expression said not a penny less.

Ten dollars stood between me and a portrait of the city I loved. My feelings said, "Buy!" My practical side said, "Walk." I hesitated, then walked away. For months after I returned from that trip I relived the decision, wishing I could take it back. The experience taught me a valuable lesson: pay more attention to feelings.

7. *Let yourself go.* Last year on a vacation in Vermont with

my family, I was walking up the steps of the state capitol building when a wave of excitement hit me. I had returned to visit my boyhood home, and I couldn't contain myself. Standing next to an old cannon, with one hand on the barrel, I began a speech: "Fellow Vermonters," I shouted to the strangers walking by, "your long-lost son has returned." As I continued my speech, the natives stared in disbelief.

What was behind my bizarre behavior? Had I gone crazy? No, I had gone truly sane. I was allowing my excitement to reach the surface and come out in action. I know I sounded silly, but I was feeling very fine.

Life has many special moments, times when your emotions are at a high pitch. Don't stifle them. Give them expression. Skip down the street instead of walking. Hug a friend you've never hugged before. Cheer at a ball game, even if you're the only one rooting for the visiting team. Sing when the band plays. Regain that lovely quality of childhood—the ability to respond to any moment.

ART ULENE, M.D.

ADDING UP TO HAPPINESS

Creative arithmetic may be the path to happiness.

Over lunch recently, an old friend and I talked about life. She admitted that she'd been lonely since her husband died. "Yet I can't complain," she said. "I had a good marriage. The kids are on their own. My job isn't exactly thrilling, but it's secure, and I retire in 15 years. So what else is there?"

What else indeed! A woman of 50—able, experienced, attractive—assuming, in effect, that her life is over. I've seen this often, and in much younger people—the resigned conviction that change is impossible. What many of us fail to realize is that it's possible at *any* age to improve the quality of our life.

It's almost never too late to do, on some scale, what you've always wanted to do. The key is to move forward, to make changes. The path many of my acquaintances have taken to greater happiness may be thought of as a kind of creative arithmetic, with additions, subtractions, multiplications and divisions. Chances are these steps will work for you, too.

Add to your life by trying something new. Remember the first-day-of-school challenge? That annual shakeup obliged you to mix, reach out, discover.

When I consider which of my friends seem happiest, most alive, I observe they're the ones who are constantly expanding their skills, interests and knowledge.

Add to your life by turning limitations into opportunities. If your life has a built-in constraint, struggle against it or use it to your advantage. When an industrial accident confined

Martin to a wheelchair, he was overwhelmed by the feeling of uselessness. One day I asked if I could give his telephone number to my daughter's teacher, in case there should be an emergency when I couldn't be reached. Soon he was performing a similar service for other working mothers. Word got around, and now he runs an answering service. The money he earns helps pay for extras his pension wouldn't cover. "Above all," he says, "I'm *doing* something, and touching other people's lives."

Subtract from your life possessions that are a burden, activities you no longer enjoy. When I was growing up I admired my mother's wedding china, which stood in a cupboard and was brought out only for dusting. "Someday this will be yours," Mother said. During my young–married years, when I longed to entertain with style, that fine china remained in her cabinet. When it all came to me last year, I realized that at this stage of my life I don't want possessions requiring special care. So I passed the china on to my daughters. They're delighted; I'm relieved of a chore.

Multiply your points of contact with other people. My life has been enhanced since I began trying to know people whose assumptions and life–styles are unlike mine. For example, because I cultivate friendships with the children of friends, I have been introduced to music, poetry and ideas I otherwise would never have understood.

Multiply your connections with the life around you. "My wife was the social one," Philip told me. "After she died, I was terribly lonely. Then it occurred to me that I meet lots of people every day. I just hadn't been *seeing* them." He struck up a conversation about fly tying with the hardware–store manager and discovered a shared interest; the two men have since gone on several trout–fishing expeditions.

Divide your responsibilities into manageable units and delegate some of those units to others. Living well is partly a matter of making wise choices and compromises. If you want more time, more freedom or simply more help, accept the fact that some things won't be done the way you'd like. For instance, you can divide home chores among all family members, even if this means a lower standard of cooking and cleaning.

My friend Connie, who returned to her profession in middle age, arranged to share home duties with her husband on an alternating basis: each takes total responsibility for shopping, meal preparation and laundry every other month. When I asked how things were going, Connie laughed. "His cooking runs from flavorless to terrible. But I honestly don't mind. That month of freedom is so marvelous!"

Divide seemingly intractable problems into segments that can be tackled one at a time. Jenny left college, over her parents' objections, to marry a musician. Two years and two children later, he vanished, leaving her with a mountain of unpaid bills. "I used to lie in bed mornings," she told me, "unable to face the day." She began to gain strength when, instead of contemplating the whole discouraging picture, she isolated priorities.

Convinced that her best hope lay in completing her education, she listed things to be done, one at a time. "Sell car for money to tide us over. Find out about educational loans. Reapply to Boston University. Find apartment in safer neighborhood. Find good day-care center. Write Mom and Dad. Get in touch with creditors and arrange to pay when I can." By the time she contacted her parents, who'd cut off communication when she married, Jenny couldn't help but impress them with her resourcefulness.

Raise your effort level to the nth power. I used to wonder why TV advertisers repeat the same commercial so often. But of course repetition, intensification, has a special force. The principle of raising to the nth power works in all areas of life. Take home decoration. For years I've collected wicker. Scattered through the house, it added up to very little. Yet when I gathered every bit in one room, massing the rattan furniture and covering one wall with baskets, the impact was stunning.

In human relationships, where it matters most, intensification of effort may produce important gains — as it did for my friend Paul. He lives far from his mother's nursing home. Though he regularly sent long, newsy letters, his mother was always querulous when he telephoned. "I was beginning to wonder if I *had* a son" was her usual greeting. Paul would protest he'd just written; she would insist she'd had no word for weeks. So he gave up the letters, concluding that his mother's concentration wasn't equal to them. Now he sends a daily greeting, very short. Sometimes it's just a postcard, a snapshot, a note saying, "Thinking of you." He never misses a day — and the change in his mother's attitude has been remarkable.

Happiness is always an individual matter, and so is the path to happiness. To live better, you surely won't pursue all the courses suggested. If your problem is inertia, boredom or loneliness, you'll benefit most by adding or multiplying. If your days are too frenetic, you may need to subtract or divide. The most important thing, if you're not satisfied now, is to *act*.

FREDELLE MAYNARD

HAPPINESS—IT'S ONLY NATURAL

Many of the current myths about human behavior are just that—myths. Psychiatrists, social workers, even ministers and educators have been instrumental in establishing concepts that ought to be challenged. For the simple fact is this: <u>You can choose to think and feel as you desire.</u>

Here are five of the more common myths routinely put forth by human-behavior "experts"—plus several strategies for overcoming these myths on your way to a new, happier mode of living.

It is Only Natural to Be Depressed, Angry, Guilty. Isn't it time someone stood up and exclaimed, "Who says that adults have to be unhappy?" For it is *not* "only natural" to be depressed and miserable. It is, in fact, "only neurotic!" The natural state of human beings is a healthy and happy one. Most of us, as children, were spontaneous and cheerful. And then we *learned* our self-defeating behavior patterns.

It Takes a Long Time to Change a Habit. If you believe that the process of change is going to take a long time, then it will. But if you work at living your life a moment—instead of a decade—at a time, then you can cope with your problems.

I used to be a madman in traffic jams, hollering every time the cars backed up. I decided in a moment to change my behavior, and then simply carried out my decision. This is not to suggest that all change can be accomplished in a split second; but, *please*, stop believing that you must wait a long time in order to be different. By saying to yourself, "It's easy and I can do it...," you'll soon be on your way to eradicating your problem.

You Have to Work on Yourself and Your Relationships to Be Happy. In fact, you may be working too hard. Happiness comes from doing things, rather than wondering if you're doing the *right* things. When you make life hard work by constantly searching for happiness, it will elude you. An old proverb says it all: "Happiness is a journey, not a destination."

Similarly, if you're always working on your relationships, trying to understand the other person, analyzing every move, you'll probably miss the very thing you want. That is, the simple *happiness* which flows from every normal activity in life—if you just let it happen.

The Answers to Your Problems Are Located in Your Past. The most you can get from lengthy excursions into your past is a letdown. But the answers to your current problems are available to you right now. Begin by erasing all traces of self-pity that make you blame your past for what you are today. Whatever your past, you'll have to make decisions *now* if you want your present to be happier.

External Factors Made You What You Are Today. People often cite the fact that they were a middle child, or that they lived in a ghetto, or that they were born during a depression, as the reason for their present unhappiness. That's because people look for excuses to explain their self-defeating behavior. All "externals," of course, are just that—excuses.

Once you see these factors as simply the unchangeable realities of your earlier life, rather than problems, you can put the responsibility for change where it belongs: on you today, and not on your background. How to go about it? Here are seven suggestions that should help.

1. Eliminate all *roles* that you've adopted in your life; behave as you want to rather than in terms of how you feel you're *supposed* to. There is no "right" way for people to

behave. Be *you* each moment and rid yourself of roles.

2. Take constructive risks in your life. If you've always been shy and reserved, introduce yourself to a stranger. If you want to tell your mother how you feel about her behavior, do it. Most risks involve no personal danger, only anxiety. And you will find that the more you muster the courage to do the things you truly want for yourself, however risky, the more effective you will become at living happily.

3. Eliminate all blame sentences from your vocabulary. Stop saying "They're to blame" for *your* unhappiness. Replace blame sentences such as "She made me feel bad," with "I made myself feel bad when I heard what she said."

4. Be assertive. You're an adult, responsible for your own life. You never need ask anyone how you ought to lead that life. While you may want to see how your behavior will affect people, that doesn't mean you must seek their permission.

5. Several times a day, stop thinking and analyzing, and let your brain slip into neutral. Just as the body needs rest and exercise periods, so does the mind.

6. Stop looking outside yourself for validation of your worth, beauty, intellect and personality. When you fish for compliments, ask yourself if *you* are satisfied with your performance or looks. If so, ask yourself why you need anyone else to say so. You'll soon discover that the less approval you seek, the more you'll receive.

7. Decide to appreciate life even when naysayers and grumps are determined to drag you down. Surround yourself with happy faces. And stop feeling it is *your* responsibility to change those who insist on being unhappy.

Your *own expectations* are the key to this whole business of mental health. If you *expect* to be happy, healthy and fulfilled in life, then most likely it will work out that way.

WAYNE W. DYER

BE ALL YOU CAN BE

One of America's wisest counselors offers a proven program for success and happiness.

Fifty years of listening to troubled people has made me familiar, I think, with just about every human problem under the sun. But there's one so prevalent that I consider it the basic human sickness. It's the problem of the person who is living far below his potential and knows it; who is deeply unhappy, but can't seem to do anything about it.

Usually, from where the counselor sits, the person's difficulties don't seem so overwhelming — but the sufferer is convinced he can't cope with them. Although he seems to have normal intelligence, adequate education and all the necessary attributes for successful living, he can't summon them to his aid. His life is blurred, out of focus, without power or purpose.

Always, you find three deadly characteristics in such people: inertia, self-doubt and aimlessness. One autumn day, walking alone around our local golf course (I was hoping to scare up some sermon ideas), I came upon a young man raking leaves off a green. I knew him slightly, and I asked how things were going. He shrugged. "As you can see," he said, "I'm not getting anywhere."

"Where do you want to get?" I asked.

He looked at me glumly. "I don't really know," he said.

"What do you do best?" I asked. He shook his head. "I'm not sure that I'm much good at anything."

"Well, what gives you the most satisfaction?"

He frowned. "No special thing."

"Look," I said. "I've asked you three of the most important questions anyone can be asked, and I've had three completely fuzzy answers. When you go home tonight, I want you to sit down with paper and pencil, and don't get up until you've answered my questions. Then let's meet here tomorrow at this time, and we'll take it from there."

Somewhat hesitantly, he agreed. When we met the next day, he told me that he liked to work with his hands, not his head; that he thought he might have some mechanical ability; and that what he wanted most in life was some sense of purpose or direction. Shortly thereafter, he got a job in a roofing-materials factory. Did he become president of the company? No, but today he is a foreman, living a happy and productive life. All he needed was a push to stop leading an unfocused life.

I meet people like that young man so frequently that I have developed a set of guidelines to help anyone, young or old, who feels the need to bring himself into sharper focus. There are eight points in all, and they add up to quite a stiff course in self-discipline. But anyone who makes a sustained effort to apply them will become a happier, more forceful, more effective person.

1. *Pinpoint your primary goal in life.* It's not enough to say, "I want to be happy" or "I want to make money" or "I want to be a better person." You must determine *exactly* what you want, and when. You need to say, "I intend to be a registered nurse in three years," or sales manager of this company, or editor of this newspaper, or buyer for that store, in four, five, or six years.

Write down a short summary of your goal and the achievement date; put it beside your bed and read it aloud to yourself every morning when you wake up. Vagueness is the invariable hallmark of the unfocused mind. Get rid of it.

2. *Use imagination to fan desire.* There's no use pinpointing a goal in life unless you want it enormously. Daydreams and

wistful wishes are not enough; there must be intense, burning desire. Nobody can put this hunger into you; you have to develop it yourself by constant, vivid imagining of the benefits that achieving your goal will bring. Ask anyone who has achieved outstanding success in any field. He will tell you that clarity of purpose and intensity of desire are the chief ingredients of the magic formula. Unless you care, you won't get there.

3. *Expect to pay for what you get.* If you set a high goal, you will have to pay a high price. You will have to work, take chances, make sacrifices, endure setbacks. You won't be able to afford the luxury of laziness or the delights of frequent distraction. When setting your goal, remember that unless you're willing to pay the price you're wasting your time.

4. *Send the right signals to your unconscious mind.* This is crucial. The unconscious is a great dynamo, but it is also a computer that has to be properly programmed. If fear thoughts, worry thoughts, failure thoughts are constantly channeled into the unconscious, nothing very constructive is going to be sent back. But if a clear, purposeful goal is steadfastly held in the conscious mind, the unconscious will eventually accept it and begin to supply the conscious mind with plans, ideas, insights, and the energies necessary to achieve that goal.

5. *Be willing to fail—temporarily.* A man who made a long-term study of highly successful men in various fields told me that he noted they had only one trait in common: persistence. They kept picking themselves up and returning to the fight long after most men would have given up.

In a sermon not long ago, I condensed the life history of such a man. This man failed in business in '31. He was defeated for the state legislature in '32. He failed again in business in '34. He had a nervous breakdown in '41. He hoped to receive his party's nomination for Congress but didn't in '43. He ran for the Senate and lost in '55. He was defeated again for the Senate in '58. A hopeless loser, some people said. But Abraham Lincoln was elected President in 1860. He knew how to accept defeat — temporarily.

6. *Believe in the power of thought to change things.* It's very hard for most people to realize that the most powerful force in the world is an idea that has taken root in a human mind. But it is.

Not long ago in Australia, I met a remarkable man named Bert Walton. He told me that he had started out in life by failing at one school after another, then at one job after another. He was working for the Australian division of an American corporation — and going downhill at that — when a man came out from the parent company to talk to Australian employes. One sentence in the man's talk struck Walton with enormous impact. *You can — if you think you can.*

"I suddenly realized," Walton told me, "that the reason I was a failure was my habit of thinking of myself as a failure. The concept created the condition — not the other way round. So I decided to change the concept. I said to myself: 'I think I can become manager of this company for New South Wales. In fact, I think I can become manager for the whole of Australia.' Well, it took a long time and a lot of work, and there were a lot of setbacks, but that's the way things turned out. Then I got into the department-store business, and I said to myself, 'I think we can build this business into one of the big chains in Australia.' And eventually that happened, too. I'm a very ordinary man, but I got hold of one extraordinary idea, and hung on."

What happened to that man? The idea, like a burning glass, focused the rays of his personality on a definite goal with such intensity that hitherto inert elements burst into flame. The idea is not a new one. The Bible says over and over: "If ye have faith, nothing shall be impossible unto you." A staggering promise, certainly, but profoundly true.

7. *Never build a case against yourself.* Just last week, a man came up to me and asked if we could talk. He had a

stooped, dejected look. And he sounded defeated. "I'm a salesman," he said. "I make a living at it, but my work is of no importance. I'm depressed and miserable most of the time. Can you help me?"

"No," I said. "I can't crawl into your head and rearrange the machinery. But perhaps I can tell you how to help yourself. In the first place, stop cringing. Stand up straight. Next, stop running down your profession. In our society, salesmen are the ball bearings on which industry moves; without them, the economy would grind to a halt. Finally, why don't you stop looking at yourself from a worm's viewpoint and look at yourself from God's? You are His child. If you are important to Him — and you are — what gives you the right to go around proclaiming your unimportance?"

We talked a bit more; then he thanked me, and went away looking thoughtful. I hope he had learned, or begun to learn, the importance of not building a case against himself.

8. *Stop short-circuiting yourself with alibis.* Unfocused people do this constantly. They say, "The timing is wrong" or, "I'm not really qualified." They play the if-only game: "If only I had more money, or more education...if only I weren't so tied down..." The alibis go on and on, and they just reinforce the three deadly characteristics — inertia, self-doubt, aimlessness. To become a focused person you have to control self-limiting thoughts. "I don't believe in circumstances," George Bernard Shaw once said. "The people who get on in this world are the people who look for the circumstances they want, and if they can't find them, make them."

Plato once said that the unexamined life isn't worth living. The statement is as true today as it was 23 centuries ago. So, examine your life. If it is out of focus, make up your mind to get it into focus. And start today.

NORMAN VINCENT PEALE, D.D.

ACKNOWLEDGMENTS

Grateful acknowledgment is made to the following organizations and individuals for permission to reprint.

"Voyage of Discovery" by Doris Lund. ©1980 by The Reader's Digest Association, Inc.

"When In Doubt, Do!" by Arthur Gordon. Originally published in the October 1966 Reader's Digest. Copyright ©1966 by Arthur Gordon. Reprinted by permission of the author.

"Rx for the Midlife Crisis: Grab Your Kid and Play Hooky" (The Best Day of Our Lives) by Colleen Hartry. ©1977 by Colleen Hartry, Los Angeles Times.

This Hill, This Valley (April Answers) by Hal Borland (Lippincott).

Leslie Satran in Washburn Wis. Times.

"The Secret of Having Fun" by Eda LeShan. ©1969 by The Reader's Digest Association, Inc.

Gordon Parks.

"The Things That Count" by Elizabeth Starr Hill. ©1967 by The Reader's Digest Association, Inc.

"Simplify Your Life" by Martin E. Marty. ©1980 by The Reader's Digest Association, Inc.

"How to Get a Lot Out of a Little" (as it appeared in the November 1958 Reader's Digest) condensed from *Any Number Can Play* by Clifton Fadiman (World Publishing Co.). Copyright ©1957 by Clifton Fadiman. Reprinted by permission of Harper & Row, Publishers, Inc.

Kathryn Bacus in Woman's Day.

"Time Out for Happiness" by Elizabeth Starr Hill. ©1966 by The Reader's Digest Association, Inc.

"How to Enjoy the Happiest Day of Your Life" by Joseph F. Newton. ©1947 by Bulletin Co.

"Peace of Mind" (Prescriptions for Peace of Mind) Look. ©1971 by Cowles Communications Inc.

Book Designed by Patrice Barrett
Cover Photo Courtesy of the State of Vermont
Typeset in Romic and Times Roman